Contents

A letter from Pie Corbett

Dear colleague,

Welcome to *Stories for Writing* for the early years, featuring the following favourite picture books: *Dave and the Tooth Fairy* by Verna Allette Wilkins, *Traction Man Is Here* by Mini Grey and *Pumpkin Soup* by Helen Cooper.

These are just three of my favourite picture books and I have chosen them for *Stories for Writing* to incorporate my unique teaching system based on *Talk for Writing* to support storytelling, reading comprehension and writing in the classroom at Key Stage 1/P1–3.

If you follow the *Stories for Writing* teaching process and take advantage of the cross-curricular and extended writing activities that accompany every storybook, there is between 4–6 weeks worth of teaching materials for every story. However, as with any quality resource, this is flexible and you should feel comfortable to adapt my ideas to suit your teaching.

The Age 6–7 materials include:
- A **CD-ROM** with three interactive picture books on screen, videos of me telling my version of the story and an editable story map
- A **Planning CD-ROM** with editable lesson plans, teaching ideas and cross-curricular activities
- Special educational editions of the **picture books** for use in group/guided and independent reading sessions with inside cover notes for use in the classroom and at home
- This **Teaching Handbook**, with step-by-step guidance for every story, so that you can follow the teaching and learning sequence, including a wealth of photocopiable Resource Sheets for group and independent work

I would love to hear your experiences of using *Stories for Writing* with your children. Do come and meet me at one of my events, if you haven't already, or e-mail me to let me know how you get on. My email address is **pie@oup.com** or check out **www.OxfordPrimary.co.uk/StoriesforWriting** to find out more.

Good luck and have fun unlocking the power of storytelling in your classroom!

Best wishes,

Pie Corbett.

Pie Corbett
Talk for Writing* expert and creator of *Stories for Writing

Unlock the power of storytelling

Storytelling is at the heart of every culture. Good stories echo in the mind, acting as the blueprint for creativity and for understanding the world we live in. It is impossible to create a story out of nothing – experience of reading quality picture books, coupled with memorable storytelling, is an effective way of developing a child's imaginative world. *Stories for Writing* provides this bridge for children.

READING A STORY

Storytelling starts with the children experiencing the pleasure of a quality picture book. The class loiter with the story, discussing what happens as well as exploring and building the story's world through drama, model-making and art work. Constant rereading makes the book memorable and helps the children to internalise the language patterns. The foundations of reading are then built upon by listening to, joining in with and learning to tell another story based on the book's patterns and themes.

RETELLING A STORY

Oral storytelling is supported by a multi-sensory approach. A story map provides a visual reminder whilst actions support kinaesthetic learning, making key language patterns memorable and meaningful. The children keep retelling the tale together until they are ready to retell in groups and pairs. Revisiting the story over a number of days ensures that everyone can retell it.

CREATING A STORY

Once the oral story is deeply embedded in the children's 'story bank', the class move on to creating their own version. The old story map is annotated, changes and embellishments made, as a new class story emerges. The new story can be retold orally before the teacher uses shared writing to capture and craft it, with children's assistance. The teacher then supports the children to draw new maps, using their own ideas. They retell their own stories with a partner until their tale has been crafted and honed. The final stage is for the children to write or record their stories.

This story bridge means that when the children write, they are basing their story on both the original book and oral retelling. It is this gradual and memorable approach that ensures every child develops their own story.

Stories for Writing teaching sequence

TALKING AND READING

TALK

1

Talk together

- Use the Talk questions to tune the children into the book they are about to read by linking to children's wider knowledge and raising their curiosity.

TALK

- Before reading the book, talk about superheroes such as Batman, Superman, Ben-10, The Incredibles, etc. Make a list of some of the key features of a superhero.
- Ask: *Has anyone got an action doll they can bring in?*
- Ask the children to imagine that they are a superhero. *What special powers do they have?*

Use Resource Sheet 1 on page 60 to create a superhero.

READ

2

Share the story on screen

- Enjoy reading the storybook together on the interactive whiteboard.
- Use the Book Talk questions to explore the story in detail, imaginatively entering the story world.

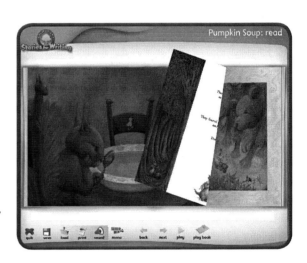

Pumpkin Soup: read

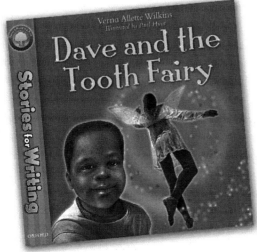

Dave and the Tooth Fairy

3

Read the picture books

- Immerse children in the story in group/guided reading sessions to deepen understanding and enjoyment.
- Encourage children to share the book at home.
- Retell the story in the children's own words using the instructions in this handbook.

Resource Sheets

Photocopiable Resource Sheets to accompany every story are highlighted throughout the teaching notes to support children's storytelling, reading comprehension and writing.

Pie Corbett's 6 steps to success!

STORYTELLING AND WRITING

TELL

Tell a new story with Pie

- Watch the video of Pie telling his new story, based on the original story idea and patterns.

- Join in telling the new story with Pie using his actions and story map.

- As children become more confident, tell the story without Pie as a class, in groups, pairs and independently.

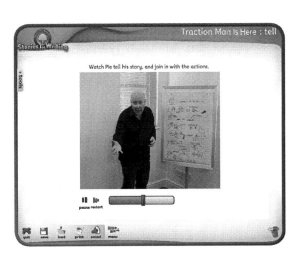

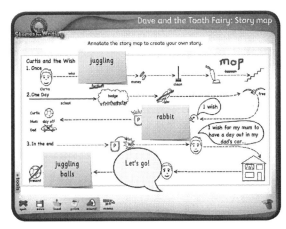

WRITE

Write a class story

- Plan a new class story using the editable story map on the CD-ROM.

- Write the shared class story using the instructions in this handbook. Turn this into a class Big Book or a wall story.

Children write their own stories

- Children create their own story maps and retell their new story.

- Children now write or record their own stories, using the shared and guided sessions as a scaffold.

Cross-curricular and Extended Writing support

Cross-curricular and Extended Writing ideas are included in the teaching notes for every story and can be integrated into your teaching at any point. These help children understand the story and inhabit the story world.

The *Stories for Writing* components

With the *Stories for Writing* CD-ROM you and the children can:

Read and share the story on screen

Listen to the story being read

Interact with the story using the interactive tool bar

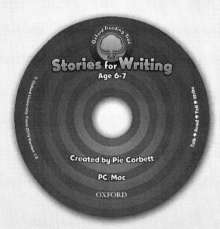

Display and edit the story maps for each book to prepare children for telling and writing their own story

Watch Pie Corbett telling his version of the story and join in with him

In the *Stories for Writing* picture books you will find:

Guidance for parents and carers on how to share the book at home on the inside front cover

Ideas for reading and sharing the story during group/guided and independent reading sessions on the inside back cover

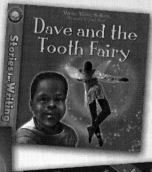

Notes about the author and illustrator for each story

Notes from Pie Corbett explaining why he chose the story

With the *Stories for Writing* **Teaching Handbook** you will find:

Step-by-step guidance for every storybook, showing how to incorporate Pie Corbett's *Stories for Writing* teaching process into your classroom

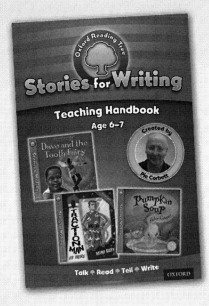

A wealth of photocopiable Resource Sheets to support children's storytelling, reading comprehension and writing

Exciting cross-curricular teaching ideas

Advice for assessing children's writing

Topic links to Oxford Reading Tree classic storybooks

The *Stories for Writing* **Planning CD-ROM** contains:

Printable weekly lesson plans using the Oxford Planning Tools

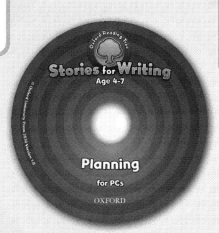

The ability to edit, adapt and save your own planning and resources

Support for cross-curricular teaching

Extra Resource Sheets – perfect for Take Home!

Ideas for mixed-age planning

Progression in *Stories for Writing*

All children need a bank of stories to draw on when creating their own. By engaging with the story; listening to it on screen; reading in pairs, in group and guided reading and at home; through exploration of character, setting and language; through role-play and drama, all children can enjoy and internalise stories.

Progression in *Stories for Writing* comes through the way the children interact with the story. This is broken up into four levels:

All ages

Imitate

The children loiter with the storybook until they are very familiar with the language patterns and have throughly entered the story's imaginative world. Use a copy of the story map for children to retell the story in their own words and pick up on familiar language patterns.

Age 4–5/Reception/P1

Simple patterned innovation

The Reception stories are retold as **simple patterned innovations** so that the children get to practise making simple changes to a story. These changes give the children ownership of the storytelling, whilst the repetitive structure of the original stories gives them the security to try out their own ideas. Encourage children to create their own stories, drawing a map. Try out the changes as a class and group retelling before the children have a go at independent retelling and writing.

Age 5–6/Year 1/P2

Complex innovation

The Year 1 stories are innovated in Pie's storytelling video. He changes characters, adds details and alters the story. The original story structure or idea remains but the children move from a simple repetitive patterned retelling to more fluent prose. Work together to create innovated class stories to retell. Encourage children to create their own stories, drawing story maps before they attempt independent retelling and writing.

Age 6–7/Year 2/P3

Invent

In Year 2 the children are focused on telling stories and using the writer's craft. The stories they explore give them the basis for creating their own adventures, characters and settings. The invented story told by Pie in his video shows the children how each story can be used to create a new one. By Year 2, children create their own stories, based on the original story idea, but craft the tale individually, drawing on the storybook as well as Pie's oral version.

Assessment in *Stories for Writing* (Age 6–7)

Formative assessment is essential in identifying the gaps in children's learning and working out how to move their reading and writing on. The *Stories for Writing* process gives children plenty of time to practise and internalise story language and structures so that by the time they record their story they can concentrate on the writer's craft.

Specific reading and writing skills are addressed through partner talk and the use of mini whiteboards in the **shared writing** sessions. **Guided reading** and **guided writing** sessions are the best place to *jump into* the reading and writing process and focus on the area that the children need more input on. Use the differentiated guided writing activities, which link to the shared writing focus, to move a group of children's writing on.

ASSESSING CHILDREN'S WRITING AND READING

The Teaching Handbook gives guidance on how to assess children's writing against a specific Assessment Focus. You will find advice on what to look for in the children's writing and ideas for moving them on, as well as suggested Assessment Focuses to help you assess the children's reading proficiency for each book.

The following chart gives an overview of the Assessment Focuses suggested for Year 2/P3 for each storybook.

Picture book	Writing Assessment Focus	Reading Assessment Focus
Dave and the Tooth Fairy	AF5: vary sentences for clarity, purpose and effect	AF3: deduce, infer or interpret information, events or ideas from text AF4: identify and comment on the structure and organisation of texts, including grammatical and presentational features at text level
Traction Man Is Here	AF1: write imaginative, interesting and thoughtful texts	AF3: deduce, infer or interpret information, events or ideas from text AF5: explain and comment on writers' use of language, including grammatical and presentational features at text level
Pumpkin Soup	AF7: select appropriate and effective vocabulary	AF1: use a range of strategies, including accurate decoding of text, to read for meaning AF3: deduce, infer or interpret information, events or ideas from text

Planning with *Stories for Writing*

The *Stories for Writing* **Planning CD-ROM** provides you with a set of editable weekly plans for each picture book, accompanied by extra Resource Sheets and cross-curricular ideas to enrich the children's reading and writing experience. It uses all the teaching ideas in the *Teaching Handbook* and provides you with a structure for your teaching that can be adapted to suit you and your children's needs.

The **Planning CD-ROM** also includes advice and suggestions for using *Stories for Writing* in a mixed-age setting.

For each book, the **Planning CD-ROM** contains:

> **A Unit overview:** a summary of the six-week teaching plan with links to the Early Years Foundation Stage objectives and the Scottish Curriculum for Excellence, assessment focuses, outcomes and cross-curricular ideas
>
> **Six Unit plans:** differentiated teaching ideas and take-home activities in step-by-step plans that can be printed out for an at-a-glance teaching prompt
>
> **Cross-curricular ideas:** exciting ideas for teaching across the wider curriculum
>
> **Resource Sheets:** an extensive set of extra Literacy and Cross-curricular activity sheets for use in the classroom or to take home

You can access all these materials through the software's easy navigation tools. The drop-down menus will allow you to select the plans you require, Resource Sheets and cross-curricular teaching ideas for each book in a few easy steps.

An example plan

Here is an example of a unit of work from the *Stories for Writing* **Planning CD-ROM**, based on the picture book *Pumpkin Soup.*

Stories for Writing headings show the stage of the process to be covered in each session

Suggestions for activities children can do at home

Session	Objectives	Summary	Starter	Main teaching	Group or Independent work (Activity with ideas for differentiation)	Plenary	Take-home activity
1 Talk	3.2 Work effectively in groups by ensuring that each group member takes a turn, challenging supporting and moving on.	Discuss turn-taking and how it feels to be left out.	Before reading the book, ask the children if they have ever cooked some food. Ask the children to role-play cooking a cake on their own. You may want to talk the process through as they do the role-play.	Talk about how things change when you do something in a group. Ask the children to think how they would cook a cake in a group of three. Encourage them to think about how to share the jobs. *Is everyone getting a fair turn?*	Ask the children to role-play leaving out one of the children in their group. Talk about how it feels to be left out. Use Resource Sheet 1 for children to record how it feels to fall out with a friend. * Write words or phrases to say how they feel. ** Use the word 'because' to try and explain why they feel that way.	Make a mind map of all the different feelings the children have written about. Talk about how these negative situations could be solved.	
2 Read (Read the story together)	6.1 Spell with increasing accuracy drawing on…spelling patterns including common inflections.	Read the story together.	Show the front cover of the book on screen. Talk about it. Ask the children what they think the story might be about.	Listen to the story all the way through. Encourage the children to join in with the reading, and share their responses at the end, asking for children's questions and observations.	Start **guided reading groups** * Listen to the story a second time and talk about their responses to the story with an adult. ** Write their personal response to *Pumpkin Soup* (Resource Sheet 2).	Go through the book. highlighting the verbs in the past tense. Choose those which just have '-ed' added, without the root word changing (stitched, filled, packed. etc.)	
3 Read (Book talk)	5.3 Know how to tackle words that are not completely decodable.	Read the story.	Read the book together, with the children joining in. Model how to break down multi-syllabic words such as 'embroidered'. Ask the children: *How do you think the animals shared out the cooking jobs at the beginning?*	Listen to the story, stopping at different points to ask the book talk questions. Discuss any additional points the children raise.	**Guided reading group** * Write their personal response to *Pumpkin Soup* (Resource Sheet 2) with adult support. ** Look at the book and think about questions/ideas they'd like to explore further.	Go through the book highlighting the past tense verbs which double the last letter when you add '-ed' (tugged, bopped, etc.) Explain that if the last letter is a consonant and the letter before is a vowel on its own, you double the last letter before adding 'ed'.	Ask the children to find more verbs that follow this rule.
4 Read (Explore the story)	7.1 Give some reasons why things happen or characters change.	Discuss how the characters feel.	Display the opening setting on screen. Ask the children to imagine going through a 'magic mirror' so they become part of the woodland setting. Follow the setting activity in the *Teaching Handbook*.	Display the pages where the characters have the fight on screen. Follow the character activity in the *Teaching Handbook*.	**Guided reading group** Use Resource Sheet 3 for the children to make puppets to act out the fight. * Work in groups of three to act out the fight with the puppets. ** Talk about how the characters feel during the first fight and how they feel at the end of the story.	Display the pages of the fight. Ask the children to work with their partner to come up with ideas about what the different characters might be thinking/saying. Use the speech/thought bubbles to scribe some of their ideas.	Children use *Planning Resource Sheet 1* to write a speech and thought bubble for each character before and after the big fight.
5 Read (Explore the story)	1.2 Tell real and imagined stories using the conventions of familiar story language.	Explore the opening.	Play: Change it! with the class (*Teaching Handbook*).	Read the first page of the book together again. Follow the Language activity in the *Teaching Handbook*.	**Guided reading group** Re-read the opening and work in pairs with mini whiteboards to innovate an opening. * Re-read the opening and play Change it! ** Have a go at composing an innovated opening to *Pumpkin Soup.*	Read the book together with the children joining in.	

Literacy objectives provide a focus for each session

Prompts for whole class, group and independent work, so you can get the most out of the materials and resources. One-star and two-star activities help you to support children to work at their own level

Objectives Chart for
Dave and the Tooth Fairy

This chart shows the Literacy Framework and Scottish Curriculum for Excellence objectives that can be covered using the teaching notes for *Dave and the Tooth Fairy* (pages 26 to 33) and the detailed planning grids on the Planning CD-ROM. The Planning CD-ROM shows how the teaching breaks down into six units of work, with five sessions in each unit.

Unit	*Stories for Writing*	Literacy Framework objectives
1	Talk Read	**1.3** Explain ideas and processes using imaginative vocabulary and non-verbal gesture to support communication. **2.3** Respond to presentations by describing characters, repeating some highlight and commenting constructively. **7.1** Draw together ideas and information from across a whole text. **8.3** Explain their reactions to texts, commenting on important aspects. **7.4** Use syntax and context to build their store of vocabulary when reading for meaning.
2	Read Tell	**4.1** Adopt appropriate roles in small or large groups and consider alternative courses of action. **8.3** Explain their reactions to texts, commenting on important aspects. **1.2** Tell real and imagined stories using the conventions of familiar story language. **3.3** Listen to each other's views and preferences.
3	Tell Write	**1.2** Tell real and imagined stories using the conventions of familiar story language. **9.1** Draw on knowledge and experience of texts in deciding and planning what and how to write. **9.3** Make adventurous word and language choices appropriate to the style and purpose of the text.
4	Write	**1.2** Retell stories, ordering events using story language. **9.1** Draw on knowledge and experience of texts in deciding and planning what and how to write. **9.4** Find and use new and interesting words and phrases, including story language. **11.1** Write simple and compound sentences and begin to use subordination in relation to time and reason. **9.2** Sustain form in narrative, including use of person and time.
5	Write	**11.1** Write simple and compound sentences and begin to use subordination in relation to time and reason. **9.4** Make adventurous word choices appropriate to the style and purpose of the text. **9.5** Select from different presentational features to suit particular writing purposes on paper and on screen. **3.1** Ensure that everyone contributes, allocate tasks, and consider alternatives and reach agreement. **3.2** Work effectively in groups by ensuring that each group member takes a turn, challenging, supporting and moving on.
6	Extended Writing	**9.4** Make adventurous word choices appropriate to the style and purpose of the text. **9.1** Drawn on knowledge and experience of texts in deciding and planning what to write. **7.1** Draw together ideas and information from across a whole text, using simple signposts in the text. **9.2** Sustain form in narrative, including use of person and time. **9.3** Maintain consistency in non-narrative, including purpose and tense.

Unit	*Stories for Writing*	Scottish Curriculum for Excellence objectives
1	Talk Read	**LIT 0-09b** I enjoy exploring events and characters in stories and other texts and I use what I learn to invent my own, sharing these with others in imaginative ways. **LIT 0-01c, LIT 0-19a** I enjoy exploring events and characters in stories and other texts, sharing my thoughts in different ways. **LIT 0-11b** I enjoy exploring and choosing stories and other texts to watch read or listen to, and can share my likes and dislikes. **LIT 0-21a** I explore sounds, letters and words, discovering how they work together, and I can use what I learn to help me as I read and write.
2	Read Tell	**LIT 0-19a** I enjoy exploring events and characters in stories and other texts, sharing my thoughts in different ways. **LIT 0-16a** To help me understand stories and other texts, I ask questions and link what I am learning with what I already know. **LIT 0-09a** Within real and imaginary situations, I share experiences and feeling, ideas and information in a way that communicates my message. **LIT 0-10a** As I listen and take part in conversations and discussions, I discover new words and phrases which I use to help me express my ideas, thoughts and feelings. **LIT 0-01c** I enjoy exploring events and characters in stories and other texts, sharing my thoughts in different ways. **LIT 0-02a** As I listen and talk in different situations , I am learning to take turns and am developing my awareness of when to talk and when to listen.
3	Tell Write	**LIT 0-07a** To help me understand stories and other texts, I ask questions and link what I am learning with what I already know. **LIT 0-09a** Within real and imaginary situations, I share experiences and feelings, ideas and information in a way that communicates my message. **LIT 0-01c** I enjoy exploring events and characters in stories and other texts, sharing my thoughts in different ways. **LIT 0-21a** I explore sounds, letters and words, discovering how they work together, and I can use what I learn to help me as I read or write. **LIT 0-01a** I enjoy exploring and playing with the patterns and sounds of language, and can use what I learn.
4	Write	**LIT 0-09a** Within real and imaginary situations, I share experiences and feelings, ideas and information in a way that communicates my message. **LIT 0-20a** I enjoy exploring and playing with the patterns and sounds of language and can use what I learn. **LIT 0-21a** I explore sounds, letters and words, discovering how they work together, and I can use what I learn to help me as I read or write. **LIT 0-21b** As I play and learn, I enjoy exploring interesting materials for writing and different ways of recording my experiences and feelings, ideas and information.
5	Write	**LIT 0-21b** As I play and learn, I enjoy exploring interesting materials for writing and different ways of recording my experiences and feelings, ideas and information. **LIT 0-21a** I explore sounds, letters and words, discovering how they work together, and I can use what I learn to help me as I read and write. **ENG 0-31a** I enjoy exploring events and characters in stories and other texts and I use what I learn to invent my own, sharing these with others in imaginative ways. **LIT 0-02a** As I listen and talk in different situations, I am learning to take turns and am developing my awareness of when to talk and when to listen. **LIT 0-07a** To help me understand stories and other texts, I ask questions and link what I am learning with what I already know.
6	Extended Writing	**LIT 0-21a** I explore sounds, letters and words, discovering how they work together, and I can use what I learn to help me as I read and write. **LIT 0-20a** I enjoy exploring and playing with the patterns and sounds of language and can use what I learn. **LIT 0-09b** I enjoy exploring events and characters in stories and other texts and I use what I learn to invent my own, sharing these with others in imaginative ways. **LIT 0-26a** Within real and imaginary situations, I share experiences and feelings, ideas and information in a way that communicates my message. **LIT 0-21b** As I play and learn, I enjoy exploring interesting materials for writing and different ways of recording my experiences and feelings, ideas and information.

Objectives Chart for *Traction Man Is Here*

This chart shows the Literacy Framework and Scottish Curriculum for Excellence objectives that can be covered using the teaching notes for *Traction Man Is Here* (pages 34 to 41) and the detailed planning grids on the Planning CD-ROM. The Planning CD-ROM shows how the teaching breaks down into six units of work, with five sessions in each unit.

Unit	*Stories for Writing*	Literacy Framework objectives
1	Talk Read	1.3 Explain ideas and processes using imaginative and adventurous vocabulary. 8.3 Explain their reactions to texts commenting on important aspects. 1.1 Speak with clarity and use appropriate intonation when reading and reciting texts. 7.5 Explore how particular words are used, including words and expressions with similar meanings. 1.3 Explain ideas and processes using imaginative and adventurous vocabulary.
2	Read Tell	8.2 Engage with books through exploring and enacting interpretations. 8.3 Explain their reactions to texts, commenting on important aspects. 1.2 Tell real and imagined stories using the conventions of familiar story language. 4.2 Present part of traditional stories, their own stories or work drawn from other areas of the curriculum for members of their own class. 4.3 Consider how mood and atmosphere are created in live or recorded performances.
3	Tell Write	1.2 Tell real and imagined stories using the conventions of familiar story language. 4.2 Present part of traditional stories, their own stories or work drawn from other areas of the curriculum for members of their own class. 9.1 Draw on knowledge and experience of texts in deciding and planning what and how to write.
4	Write	4.2 Present part of traditional stories, their own stories or work drawn form other areas of the curriculum for members of their own class. 9.1 Draw on knowledge and experience of texts in deciding and planning what and how to write. 9.4 Make adventurous word and language choices appropriate to the text and the purpose of the text. 9.2 Sustain form in narrative including use of person and time.
5	Write	9.5 Select from different presentational features to suit particular writing purposes on paper and on screen. 9.2 Sustain form in narrative including use of person and time. 1.3 Explain ideas and processes using imaginative and adventurous vocabulary. 1.1 Speak with clarity.
6	Extended Writing	7.1 Draw together ideas and information from across a whole text, using simple signposts in the text. 10.1 Use planning to establish clear sections for writing. 9.5 Select from different presentational features to suit particular writing purposes on paper and on screen. 7.5 Explore how particular words are used. 2.3 Respond to presentations by repeating some highlight and commenting constructively.

Unit	*Stories for Writing*	Scottish Curriculum for Excellence objectives
1	Talk Read	**LIT 0-09b** I enjoy exploring events and characters in stories and other texts and I use what I learn to invent my own, sharing these with others in imaginative ways. **LIT 0-01c** I enjoy exploring events and characters in stories and other texts, sharing my thoughts in different ways. **LIT 0-07a** To help me understand stories and other texts, I ask questions and link what I am learning with what I already know. **LIT 0-10a** As I listen and take part in conversations and discussions, I discover new words and phrases which I use to help me express my ideas, thoughts and feelings. **LIT 0-11a** I enjoy exploring and playing with the patterns and sounds of language and can use what I learn.
2	Read Tell	**LIT 0-01c** I enjoy exploring events and characters in stories and other texts, sharing my thoughts in different ways. **LIT 0-14a** I use signs, books or other texts to find useful or interesting information and I use this to plan, make choices or learn new things. **ENG 0-12a** explore sounds, letters and words, discovering how they work together and I can use what I learn to help me as I read and write. **LIT 0-09a** Within real and imaginary situations, I share experiences and feelings, ideas and information in away that communicates my message.
3	Tell Write	**LIT 0-07a** To help me understand stories and other texts, I ask questions and link what I am learning with what I already know. **LIT 0-09a** Within real and imaginary situations, I share experiences and feelings, ideas and information in a way that communicates my message. **LIT 0-01c** I enjoy exploring events and characters in stories and other texts, sharing my thoughts in different ways. **LIT 0-20a** I enjoy exploring and playing with the patterns and sounds of language and can use what I learn.
4	Write	**LIT 0-26a** Within real and imaginary situations, I share experiences and feelings, ideas and information in a way that communicates my message. **LIT 0-20a** I enjoy exploring and playing with the patterns and sounds of language and can use what I learn. **LIT 0-21a** I explore sounds, letters and words, discovering how they work together, and I can use what I learn to help me as I read or write. **LIT 0-21b** As I play and learn, I enjoy exploring interesting materials for writing and different ways of recording my experiences and feelings, ideas and information.
5	Write	**LIT 0-20a** I enjoy exploring and playing with the patterns and sounds of language and can use what I learn. **LIT 0-21a** I explore sounds, letters and words, discovering how they work together, and I can use what I learn to help me as I read or write. **ENG 0-31a** I enjoy exploring events and characters in stories and other texts and I use what I learn to invent my own, sharing these with others in imaginative ways. **LIT 0-04a** I listen or watch for useful or interesting information and I use this to make choices or learn new things. **LIT 0-07a** To help me understand stories and other texts, I ask questions and link what I am learning with what I already know.
6	Extended Writing	**LIT 0-04a** I listen or watch for useful or interesting information and I use this to make choices or learn new things. **LIT 0-07a** To help me understand stories and other texts, I ask questions and link what I am learning with what I already know. **LIT 0-26a** Within real and imaginary situations, I share experiences and feelings, ideas and information in a way that communicates my message. **ENG 0-31a** I enjoy exploring events and characters in stories and other texts and I use what I learn to invent my own, sharing these with others in imaginative ways.

Objectives Chart for *Pumpkin Soup*

This chart shows the Literacy Framework and Scottish Curriculum for Excellence objectives that can be covered using the teaching notes for *Pumpkin Soup* (pages 42 to 49) and the detailed planning grids on the Planning CD-ROM. The Planning CD-ROM shows how the teaching breaks down into six units of work, with five sessions in each unit.

Unit	*Stories for Writing*	Literacy Framework objectives
1	Talk Read	3.2 Work effectively in groups by ensuring that each group member takes a turn, challenging supporting and moving on. 6.1 Spell with increasing accuracy drawing on spelling patterns including common inflections. 5.3 Know how to tackle words that are not completely decodable. 7.1 Give some reasons why things happen or characters change. 1.2 Tell real and imagined stories using the conventions of familiar story language.
2	Read Tell	8.2 Engage with books through exploring and enacting interpretations. 8.3 Explain their reactions to texts, commenting on important aspects. 1.2 Tell real and imagined stories using the conventions of familiar story language. 4.2 Present part of traditional stories, their own stories or work drawn from other areas of the curriculum for members of their own class. 3.3 Listen to each other's views and preferences, agree the next steps to take and identify contributions by each group's member.
3	Tell Write	1.2 Tell real and imagined stories using the conventions of familiar story language. 4.2 Present part of traditional stories, their own stories or work drawn from other areas of the curriculum for members of their own class. 9.1 Draw on knowledge and experience of texts in deciding and planning what and how to write.
4	Write	4.2 Present part of traditional stories, their own stories or work drawn form other areas of the curriculum for members of their own class. 9.1 Draw on knowledge and experience of texts in deciding and planning what and how to write. 11.1 Compose sentences using tense consistently. 9.4 Make adventurous word and language choices appropriate to the text and the purpose of the text. 9.2 Sustain form in narrative including use of person and time.
5	Write	9.5 Select from different presentational features to suit particular writing purposes on paper and on screen. 9.2 Sustain form in narrative including use of person and time. 1.3 Explain ideas and processes using imaginative and adventurous vocabulary. 1.1 Speak with clarity.
6	Extended Writing	3.2 Work effectively in groups by ensuring that each group member takes a turn, challenging supporting and moving on. 2.3 Respond to presentations by repeating some highlight and commenting constructively. 7.5 Explore how particular words are used. 9.4 Make adventurous word and language choices appropriate to the text and the purpose of the text.

Unit	Stories for Writing	Scottish Curriculum for Excellence objectives
1	Talk Read	**LIT 0-02a** As I listen and talk in different situations, I am learning to take turns and am developing my awareness of when to talk and when to listen. **LIT 0-01b** I enjoy exploring and choosing stories and other texts to watch, read or listen to, and can share my likes and dislikes. **ENG 0-12a** I explore sounds, letters and words, discovering how they work together, and I can use what I learn to help me read and write. **LIT 0-19a** I enjoy exploring events and characters in stories and other texts, sharing my thoughts in different ways. **LIT 0-20a** I enjoy exploring and playing with the patterns and sounds of language and can use what I learn.
2	Read Tell	**LIT 0-16a** To help me understand stories and other texts, I ask questions and link what I am learning with what I already know. **LIT 0-19a** I enjoy exploring events and characters in stories and other texts, sharing my thoughts in different ways. **LIT 0-09a** Within real and imaginary situations, I share experiences and feelings, ideas and information in a way that communicates my message. **LIT 0-10a** As I listen and take part in conversations and discussions, I discover new words and phrases which I use to help me express my ideas, thoughts and feelings. **LIT 0-02a** As I listen and talk in different situations, I am learning to take turns and am developing my awareness of when to talk and when to listen.
3	Tell Write	**LIT 0-01c** I enjoy exploring events and characters in stories and other texts, sharing my thoughts in different ways. **LIT 0-21b** As I play and learn, I enjoy exploring interesting materials for writing and different ways of recording my experiences and feelings, ideas and information. **LIT 0-20a** I enjoy exploring and playing with the patterns and sounds of language and can use what I learn. **LIT 0-26a** Within real and imaginary situations, I share experiences and feelings, ideas and information in a way that communicates my message.
4	Write	**LIT 0-26a** Within real and imaginary situations, I share experiences and feelings, ideas and information in a way that communicates my message. **LIT 0-20a** I enjoy exploring and playing with the patterns and sounds of language and can use what I learn. **LIT 0-21a** I explore sounds, letters and words, discovering how they work together, and I can use what I learn to help me as I read or write. **ENG 0-12a** I explore sounds, letters and words, discovering how they work together, and I can use what I learn to help me as I read or write. **LIT 0-21b** As I play and learn, I enjoy exploring interesting materials for writing and different ways of recording my experiences and feelings, ideas and information.
5	Write	**LIT 0-20a** I enjoy exploring and playing with the patterns and sounds of language and can use what I learn. **LIT 0-21a** I explore sounds, letters and words, discovering how they work together, and I can use what I learn to help me as I read or write. **ENG 0-31a** I enjoy exploring events and characters in stories and other texts and I use what I learn to invent my own, sharing these with others in imaginative ways. **LIT 0-04a** I listen or watch for useful or interesting information and I use this to make choices or learn new things. **LIT 0-19a** I enjoy exploring events and characters in stories and other texts, sharing my thoughts in different ways.
6	Extended Writing	**LIT 0-02a** As I listen and talk in different situations, I am learning to take turns and am developing my awareness of when to talk and when to listen. **LIT 0-26a** Within real and imaginary situations, I share experiences and feelings, ideas and information in a way that communicates my message. **LIT 0-21a** I explore sounds, letters and words, discovering how they work together, and I can use what I learn to help me as I read and write. **LIT 0-20a** I enjoy exploring and playing with the patterns and sounds of language and can use what I learn.

How to use the CD-ROM

MAIN MENU

You can access all areas of the CD content through the Main menu

Select a book to get started

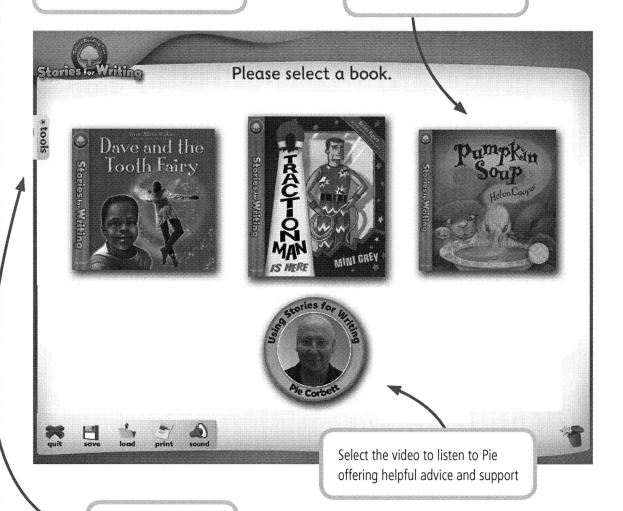

Fully interact with the stories and story maps using the toolbar

Select the video to listen to Pie offering helpful advice and support

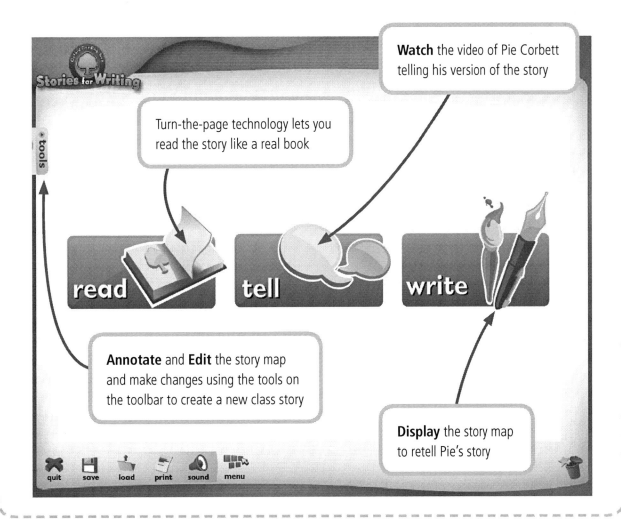

Watch the video of Pie Corbett telling his version of the story

Turn-the-page technology lets you read the story like a real book

tools

read

tell

write

Annotate and Edit the story map and make changes using the tools on the toolbar to create a new class story

Display the story map to retell Pie's story

quit   save   load   print   sound   menu

HOW TO USE THE TOOLS

Fully interact with the picture books on screen by using the toolbar.

 Drag the **speech** and **thought bubbles** and **sticky notes** to type in text that shows what a character might be saying or thinking or to annotate the text.

 Use the **zoom** tool to enlarge the illustrations so you can see more details. Depending on your whiteboard, select the page with your whiteboard stylus or finger to zoom around the page.

 Use the **highlighter** tool to identify words, phrases, sentences or punctuation in the story.

 Use the **grab** tool to move annotations on the screen.

 Use the **pen tool** to annotate the story text, write replacement synonyms, collect the children's ideas and make changes to Pie's story map.

 If you have the tool bar open and you are using an annotation tool, select the **control** tool to return to the story controls.

How to use the picture books

AT SCHOOL

The *Stories for Writing* storybooks have been chosen because they are favourite children's books with enormous potential for talking and writing. They are not books that all children could be expected to read independently, so the notes on the inside back covers of the books will help you to support children in group and guided reading sessions.

Knowing the book deeply

Pie Corbett suggests that we loiter with stories, getting to know them really well. The activities in the Read and Tell sections of *Stories for Writing* give ample opportunities to do just this. Use the question prompts, activities, role-play and drama to explore the book at many levels. Make a role-play area in your classroom and use the cross-curricular ideas so that children can engage with the story at every opportunity. The extended writing activities can be used at any point you feel appropriate.

Read together on screen

Play the storybook on screen so that the children listen to the story being read to them. You can use the story to model reading strategies and highlight words to reinforce phonic skills or strategies to remember tricky high frequency words.

Reading is not just the process of decoding and by using the storybook on screen you will discover a rich resource for reading as a writer as well as inferential and deductive questioning, which are all supported in the notes in this handbook.

Read together as a group

The notes on the inside back covers of the storybooks give guidance for group or guided reading sessions in class.

AT HOME

Children can take the special educational editions of the storybooks home with them to share what they know about the story with their parents and carers, as well as to enjoy reading the story with them.

The notes on the inside front covers give parents and carers ideas for reading and exploring the storybook with their child. Children are not expected to be able to read the book independently but rather to enjoy retelling the story, talking about the pictures, characters and events, and spending time doing the suggested activities together.

Why Pie chose the picture books

DAVE AND THE TOOTH FAIRY

- This story is about something that every child can identify with.
- I loved tip-toeing into my children's room and hiding a coin under their pillow when they were asleep.
- It is a gentle exploration of a grandfather and grandson's relationship.
- The realistic, detailed illustrations bring magic into the real world.

TRACTION MAN IS HERE

- Boys and girls love *Traction Man Is Here* because it is funny and a bit like a comic.
- The story explores the imaginative play of a young boy and his favourite toy with great humour. It is full of ridiculous things.
- The stereotype of the superhero is twisted as his adventures take place amongst everyday household objects.
- *Traction Man Is Here* is a series of rescue episodes. This is a great model for young writers.

PUMPKIN SOUP

- *Pumpkin Soup* appeals to me because it explores the ups and downs of friendship.
- Helen Cooper draws you into the story by weaving the pictures and words together.
- I like the way the illustrations are like something out of a fairy tale.
- *Pumpkin Soup* helps children understand the consequences of behaving badly and the importance of compromise in a relationship.

- The characters in *Pumpkin Soup* have to change to solve their problem. This is great for early storytelling and writing.

About the storybook authors and illustrators

DAVE AND THE TOOTH FAIRY

Verna Allette Wilkins was born in Grenada.

- She founded Tamarind Books in 1987 to provide books that represent children of all colours and abilities in real situations.
- She has written over 30 picture books and biographies.
- Verna now lives in London.

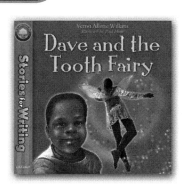

TRACTION MAN IS HERE

Mini Grey has worked as a theatre designer and a primary school teacher.

- She won the 2007 Kate Greenaway Medal for *The Adventures of the Dish and the Spoon*.
- She got her name after being born in a Mini Cooper in a car park!
- She says that *Changes* by Anthony Browne was one of the picture books that made her want to write and illustrate for children.
- She uses real life objects in her pictures, such as tomatoes and biscuits!

PUMPKIN SOUP

Helen Cooper was born in 1963.

- Helen Cooper won the 1998 Kate Greenaway Medal for *Pumpkin Soup*.

- She grew up in Cumbria and got her milk fresh from the nearby farm everyday.

- She wrote *Delicious*, which has the same characters in as *Pumpkin Soup*, to inspire children to cook at home and understand what it is like to cook for someone who is a fussy eater!

Dave and the Tooth Fairy

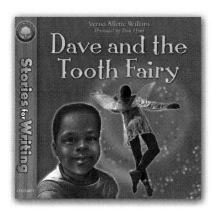

TALK

- Before reading the book, ask children to talk about their Tooth Fairy stories. Have they lost any of their teeth? Have they ever written to the Tooth Fairy? Ask: *What do you think the Tooth Fairy looks like?*

- Ask the children to make up a new type of fairy. *How might it move? What is its job? What does it look like?*

Use Resource Sheet 1 on page 50 for the children to create a new fairy.

READ

1 Read the story together

- Select *Dave and the Tooth Fairy* on the CD-ROM.

- Click on *Read* to listen to the story being read from beginning to end without interruption.

- Enjoy the story and let the children discuss any aspect they are interested in.

- Let the children raise their own questions.

2 Book Talk

- Reread the story and make sure it is on display whilst you explore these open questions. Encourage paired and group discussions. Interact with the text using the zoom, sticky notes and annotating tools to record the children's responses and ideas.

  o *Who is the most important character in the story and why?*

  o *How would you solve Dave's problem?*

  o *Was Dave right to take Grandad's teeth?*

  o *Who is happiest at the end of the book?*

  o *How would you describe Grandad?*

- Stop at points in the book and ask:

  o *How do you think Grandad felt when he saw his own teeth underneath Dave's pillow?*

  o *Look through the book and find the silent and noisy pictures.*

  o *Do you think Dave will tell Grandad what he did with the teeth?*

  o *How do you think Afiya's wings work?*

  o *What do you think Afiya thought when she found only one tooth?*

Use Resource Sheet 2 on page 51 for the children to note a personal response to the story.

 **READ**

3 Explore the story

Setting: night time in the house

- Look at the night time pictures. Use the magnifying glass to zoom in on Grandad and ask the children to imagine they are in that room.

- Use questioning to create an atmospheric description of the room. *What can they hear? What can they see? What are they feeling or thinking?*

- Encourage the children to create their own atmospheric descriptions.

Characters: Dave, Grandad and Afiya

- Take each character in turn and read through the story, collecting ideas about each of them.

- Ask the children to talk about what each character is thinking as they creep around the house at night.

- *What would Grandad say to Grandma about what happened? How do Dave's feelings change during the story?*

 Use Resource Sheet 3 on page 52 for children to collect information about Dave and Afiya from the book.

Word and Language Games: adjectives

- Read the book together again, this time concentrating on the adjectives. Focus on the adjectives that make comparisons (e.g. *an enormous comb*).

- Encourage the children to think of synonyms for the different adjectives to use in their writing.

- **Game: Word line up.** Ask the children to help you make a list of words to describe size (*tiny, minuscule, huge, enormous*). Write them onto cards. Can they put them in order?

Role-and Drama

 Use Resource Sheet 4 on page 53 for children to practise using adjectives.

- *Was Dave dishonest to try and trick the Tooth Fairy?* Organise the children into two lines – one line will give reasons why Dave was dishonest and the other will say why he wasn't.

- Ask a child to be Dave. Send 'Dave' between the two lines to listen to the reasons. Ask 'Dave' to say whether he thinks he was dishonest or not.

4 Guided/group and independent reading

- You will find ideas for parents/carers to use *Dave and the Tooth Fairy* with their child at home on the inside front cover of the storybook.

- You will find ideas for guided/group reading using *Dave and the Tooth Fairy* on the inside back cover of the storybook.

An extract from *Dave and the Tooth Fairy*, by Verna Allette Wilkins, with kind permission from Random House Children's Books

David Alexander Curtis had a wobbly tooth. A very wobbly tooth.

He wibbled it and wobbled it backwards and forwards, but it wouldn't come out.

5 Reading as a Writer

Return to the book and use it to explore the questions below, beginning to think about what might be needed to create your own version.

Plot

- Discuss with the children the kind of story *Dave and the Tooth Fairy* is. It is a wishing story.

- *What else could Dave wish for?* He could wish for: a football, a Frisbee, a new toy, etc.

- *Which other magical creature could be involved?* An elf, a wizard, a genie, etc.

Setting

- *Where is Dave and the Tooth Fairy set?* It is set in Dave's house and the main action happens at night time.

- *Where else could Dave and the Tooth Fairy be set?* At Grandad's house, a friend's house, camping, etc.

Character

- *How many main characters are there in Dave and the Tooth Fairy?* There are three – Dave, Grandad and Afiya.

- Talk about how Dave's plan to use Grandad's teeth so he could get money for the kite could have gone wrong if Grandad hadn't intervened.

Language

- Reread the story and look at how the night is described. (*It was a clear, warm night. She heard the hoot of an owl far away, and a bat came close as she flew.*)

- *Are there any other words that we could use to describe the night?* (*It was a blustery, chilly night; It was a stormy, wet night.*) Invent similes to describe the moon and the stars.

6 Other stories to read

Wishing stories

- *My wobbly tooth must not ever never fall out* by Lauren Child
- *The Magic Bed* by John Burningham
- *Across the Blue Mountains* by Emma Chichester Clark
- *Cinderella* by The Brothers Grimm

Stories written by Verna Allette Wilkins

- *Are we there yet?*
- *Boots for a Bridesmaid*
- *Kim's Magic Tree*
- *Toyin Fay* (the follow on from *Dave and the Tooth Fairy*)

7 Links to Oxford Reading Tree classic stories Stages 6–9

- Grandparents: *Homework* (Stage 6), *The Motorway* (Stage 7)
- Wishes: *The Evil Genie* (Stage 8), *Superdog* (Stage 9), *The Litter Queen* (Stage 9)
- Fairytale characters: *Kipper and the Giant* (Stage 6), *The Laughing Princess* (Stage 6), *The Evil Genie* (Stage 8)

DAVE AND THE TOOTH FAIRY

TELL

1 Imitate: *Dave and the Tooth Fairy*

- The children need to fully understand and internalise the story before they move on to telling Pie's innovated story.

- As a class, join in with the story.

- Encourage children to take different parts, echo the story using expression or ask the children to try retelling the story in groups or pairs.

- Emphasise the night time as you retell the story to highlight how Dave tries to solve his problem and how Grandad comes to the rescue.

- Use an enlarged copy of the *Dave and the Tooth Fairy* story map on Resource Sheet 5 for children to retell the story in their own words, or draw your own.

> Use Resource Sheet 5 on page 54 to retell *Dave and the Tooth Fairy* as a class.

2 Innovate: Pie Corbett's story

- Tell the class that they are going to learn how to tell a new story, *Curtis and the Wish*. It is similar to *Dave and the Tooth Fairy*, but some things have changed.

- Click on *Tell* to play the video of Pie Corbett telling the story of *Curtis and the Wish* using his story map and actions. Encourage the class to join in.

- Replay the video as many times as needed. As the children become more confident, gradually turn down the volume so that they retell the story without Pie's voice.

- Ask the children to retell the story as a class, then in groups or pairs, before they have a go on their own.

- Retelling is not a memory game. Most children will need to see a story map, do the actions and possibly use objects, to retell the story clearly.

- An enlarged photocopy of the story map, or your own version of it, should always be displayed.

> Use Resource Sheet 6 on page 55 to retell *Curtis and the Wish*. Some children may want to create their own story maps. Resource Sheet 7 on page 56 shows Pie's story script.

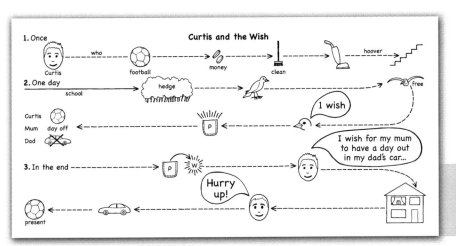

A story map of Pie's innovated story, *Curtis and the Wish*

WRITE

1 Planning together

- Click on *Write* to use Pie's story map to help you invent a shared class story.

- Make appropriate changes and practise each one as you add them to the story map on screen or on a flip chart. In this way your own version of the story will gradually develop.

- Ensure the children are involved in this process, using partner talk or mini whiteboards to compose their ideas.

- Ideas for changes include:

  o Create new characters, e.g. Zappo the Tooth Fairy, Granny Jam Jam.

  o Create a new problem, e.g. Ailsa can't sleep and worries that the Tooth Fairy won't come.

  o Create a new setting, e.g. Ailsa stays overnight at Granny Jam Jam's house.

  o Add descriptions, e.g. the bed was lumpy and hard. It was the most uncomfortable bed ever.

  o Add adjectives to show comparisons, e.g. the tiniest, the most difficult, the unhappiest.

- Retell the new story as a class, in groups and then in pairs.

2 Shared writing

- Once the children know the new class story, move into shared writing.

- Retell the class story and as you write embellish it.

  o Keep rereading to ensure the flow of the story is maintained.

  o Make occasional errors or use a weak word to demonstrate editing skills.

  o Encourage children to give you the best words they can think of.

  o Draw out what the characters might be thinking at different points in the story.

  o Ask the children to work in pairs using their mini whiteboards to describe these emotions.

  o Tell the children that you will be looking out for their use of thoughts and feelings to describe different characters in their writing.

3 Recording children creating their own stories

- Lead children through developing their own map based on this story.

- In pairs, encourage them to tell and retell their version before recording it.

- Work with groups, pairs or individual children to help them record stories at their own level.

Children can:

o dictate to an adult who scribes

o record their story using a microphone

o video their story with a digital camera

o perform to a group

o write a group text

o write with support

o write independently, with annotations in consultation with an adult

o write independently.

WRITE

4 Guided writing

Focus: vary sentences for clarity, purpose and effect (AF5)

- Some children may need help with this focus and this session should only occur once the children have written some of their own story.

- Read the pages where Grandad wakes up at night.

- Model how to vary some of the sentence starts by using an adverb or time word connective, such as '*Slowly, he picked it up.*'

- Experiment by trying short and long sentences to create different effects.

- You can differentiate this session for less confident and more confident children.

  - o Work on the text with a group and concentrate on improving the sentence starts together.

  - o Challenge children to use thoughts and feelings in their story to create a fuller picture of their characters.

5 Assessing children's writing

Focus: vary sentences for clarity, purpose and effect (AF5)

- Focus on how the children control their sentences. Do they all start the same way or in a variety of ways? Confident writers will be able to write about their characters' emotions and thoughts in such a way that we learn more about them. For less confident writers, the action remains the focus.

- Use *I can* statements to encourage children to evaluate their writing, for example: *I can use adverbs and time words to start my sentences.*

- All children can improve their sentence structure by:

  - o Reading their work aloud to make sure it makes sense.

  - o Highlighting their sentence starts and seeing if they overuse the same ones.

  - o Thinking about using time connectives and adverbs at the beginning of sentences to move the story on.

✏ EXTENDED WRITING

1 Under the sofa, what could you see?

- Display the pages with Dave searching under the sofa for his tooth.

- Show the children a bag with a variety of objects in it and tell them that you found these things under your sofa.

- Model describing them. For example, *one dusty, chipped bone china cup with flowers on it,* etc.

- Encourage the children to describe each item to their partner.

- Make a list poem of the things you found under your sofa. For example, *Under my old sofa I found… one dusty, chipped bone china cup with flowers on it,* and so on.

 Use Resource Sheet 8 on page 57 for the children to write their list poem.

2 An interview for the job of Tooth Fairy

- Tell the children that the Tooth Fairy agency is looking for a new Tooth Fairy to replace Afiya.

- Read the job description to the children on Resource Sheet 9 and ask the children to talk about any other skills that a Tooth Fairy might need.

- Tell the children that they are going to take turns to be the interviewer for the Tooth Fairy job, but first they must write the questions.

 Use Resource Sheet 9 on page 58 to help the children compose their five questions to ask at the interview.

3 Write a thank you note to the Tooth Fairy

- Tell the children that they are going to write a thank you note from Dave. He should say what he used his money for and the fun he had.

- Model writing a thank you letter before the children write their own.

- Leave a tiny letter of reply for the children to read!

4 Afiya's diary entry

- Tell the children that they are going to write a diary entry in role as Afiya. They need to think how she might feel after all that flying. *What did Afiya make of the disappearing teeth? Does she know that Dave tried to trick her?*

 Use Resource Sheet 10 on page 59 to help children write their diary entry.

5 Fairy wand list poem

- Make up a list poem about what you would do with a fairy's wand, for example:

With my fairy wand I would –
Turn clouds into candy floss,
Turn the sun into a beach ball.

Art

- Talk about the illustrator's use of perspective, colour and light and dark. *How does this affect the story?*
- Ask the children to draw Grandad or an older person they know.

Design and Technology

- Look at the different kites in the kite shop. Discuss how the different shapes have been used to catch the wind.
- Design a kite using a fixed frame like Dave's kite.
- Make a model of the kite using lolly sticks and tissue paper.

Geography

- Look at the map of the world in Afiya's office. Can the children see the Tooth Fairy flight paths?
- Use a large-scale map of the world and help the children draw the flight paths from one country to another.

Maths

- Talk about the different shapes of the kites.
- Give the children limited shapes to make kite patterns with.

Music

- Create a night time atmosphere using voice and gentle percussion sounds.
- Compose music for Afiya's return flight: *Back she flew, over trees, over hills to Tooth Fairyland. It was her fastest flight ever.*

PE

- Make up a game using the commands *over, under, faster, slower, tiptoes* and *fly,* to tell the children how to move around the room and apparatus.

PSHE

- Talk about what it is like to lose something. *Have the children ever lost anything very important to them?*
- Talk about how it feels to lose something when you know you'll get in trouble for having lost it. Help the children to come up with words to describe how it makes them feel to be in this tricky situation.
- Help the children to discuss how their bodies help them know their emotions. They might feel hot when they are embarrassed or have butterflies in their tummies when they are excited or scared. Talk about how this is perfectly natural and helps us understand our emotions.

Role-play area

- Use drapes to create a fairy cavern.
- Put up a post box so children can send letters to different fairies.

Science

- What materials are good to use when making a kite?
- Look at kites and talk about how the materials to make them need to be strong and light to catch the wind.
- Test the qualities of different fabrics that you might use to make a kite from.

> **Check out the *Stories for Writing* Planning CD-ROM for week-by-week literacy plans, exciting cross-curricular ideas and extra resource sheets.**

DAVE AND THE TOOTH FAIRY

Traction Man Is Here

TALK

- Before reading the book, talk about superheroes such as Batman, Superman, Ben-10, The Incredibles, etc. Make a list of some of the key features of a superhero.

- Ask: *Has anyone got an action doll they can bring in?*

- Ask the children to imagine that they are a superhero. *What special powers do they have?*

Use Resource Sheet 1 on page 60 to create a superhero.

READ

1 Read the story together

- Select *Traction Man Is Here* on the CD-ROM.

- Click on *Read* to listen to the story being read from beginning to end without interruption.

- Enjoy the story and let the children discuss any aspect they are interested in.

- Let the children raise their own questions.

2 Book Talk

- Reread the story and make sure it is on display whilst you explore these open questions. Make this session exciting and dynamic by encouraging paired and group discussions and interact with the text using the zoom, sticky notes and annotating tools to record the children's responses and ideas.

  o *How do you think the boy felt when he got the toy he had hoped for?*

  o *Who do you think this book is about?*

  o *How long do you think the story lasts?*

  o *How would you describe Traction Man's sidekick Scrubbing Brush?*

  o *What might scare Traction Man?*

- Discuss the illustrations and what they tell us, makes us feel or think. How do the pictures add to the story?

- Stop at points in the book and ask:

  o *What do you notice in this picture?*

  o *How do you think Traction Man feels when he gets the knitted romper suit from Granny?*

  o *Let's think of some words to describe how Traction Man moves, speaks or feels here.*

  o *What could the next Traction Man episode be about?*

Use Resource Sheet 2 on page 61 for children to note a personal response to the story.

 **READ**

③ **Explore the story**

Setting: underwater in the sink

- Display the pages showing Traction Man diving in the sink. Zoom in on the underwater world.

- Work together to describe or name the different sea creatures and scribe them on the page, for example *Bacon-eel, Crumbfish, Drifting spaghetti-weed.*

- Ask the children to choose one detail of the underwater world to try to describe in detail to their partner.

Characters: stereotypes

- Choose a page and ask: *What is going on here? How can Traction Man help?*

- Talk about how Traction Man might talk to the characters who are in trouble. Model Traction Man's stereotypical superhero talk: *Never fear Scrubbing Brush! I will rescue you.* Encourage the children to act out dialogue and experiment using different voices for the characters.

- Ask children to think of words to describe how the characters speak. *Does Traction Man proclaim, shout or snarl? Do the Dollies whimper or cry?*

> Use Resource Sheet 3 on page 62 for the children to write dialogue, using powerful words instead of *said*.

Word and Language Games: capital letters

- Read the book again and notice how capital letters are used to show names.

- Make a list of the names of all the characters and talk about how these words are usually used.

- **Game: River of Doom.** *Traction Man has to cross the deep River of Doom.* Model some ideas of how he could do it, for example, he could swing across the river on a string. Make a list of ways that Traction Man could cross the river.

Role-play and Drama

- Ask the children to work in pairs and think of questions to hot-seat Traction Man.

- Ask the children to work in a small group to act out one of Traction Man's adventures. Encourage them to add another villain.

- Set up an area where a few dolls can become action heroes/heroines. Encourage the children to invent mini adventure stories using the dolls.

- Role-play Mum and Dad talking with Gran after the story has ended.

④ **Guided/group and independent reading**

- You will find ideas for parents/carers to use *Traction Man Is Here* with their child at home on the inside front cover of the storybook.

- You will find ideas for guided/group reading using *Traction Man Is Here* on the inside back cover of the storybook.

> An extract from *Traction Man Is Here*, by Mini Grey, with kind permission from Random House Children's Books

Traction Man is guarding some toast.

5 Reading as a Writer

Return to the book and use it to explore the questions below, beginning to think about what might be needed to create your own version.

Plot

- Discuss with the children the kind of story *Traction Man Is Here* is. It is a series of action episodes that make one adventure story.

- *Who else could be a baddie?* The evil Dr Glove, The Knitted Scarf of Doom, etc.

- *Which other heroes/sidekicks could join him?* Super Stan and Tiny Ted, Marvellous Mary and Sock Boy, etc.

- *What other ways could he travel?* By super-powered soup ladle, spring-propelled slinky, etc.

Setting

- *Where is the story set?* It is set in various locations in and around the home and at Granny's house.

- *Where else could the story be set?* At the supermarket, at school, at the park, etc.

Character

- *How many main characters are there in the story?* There are three main characters – Traction Man, Scrubbing Brush and the boy.

- Discuss how the boy creates Traction Man's adventures. He is telling the story from his imaginary play.

Language

- Reread the story. *Can you spot words that tell us how the action is happening?* (For example, zooming, jumps, guarding, volunteered, diving, etc.)

- *Are there any other words that we could use to say how the action is happening?* (For example, exploding, crashing, cheering, exploring, defending, etc.)

6 Other stories to read

Episodic stories

- ○ *Where are you Blue Kangaroo?* by Emma Chichester Clark
- ○ *Amazing Grace* by Mary Hoffman
- ○ *The Three Little Pigs* by Charlotte Voake
- ○ *Where's Julius?* by John Burningham

Stories written by Mini Grey

- ○ *Egg Drop*
- ○ *The Adventures of the Dish and the Spoon*
- ○ *Biscuit Bear*
- ○ *The Pea and the Princess*

7 Links to Oxford Reading Tree classic stories Stages 6–9

- Adventures: *Land of the Dinosaurs* (Stage 6), *Submarine Adventure* (Stage 7), *Viking Adventure* (Stage 8), *Victorian Adventure* (Stage 8), *Egyptian Adventure* (Stage 8), *The Quest* (Stage 9)

- Heroes: *A Ship in Trouble* (Stage 6), *Flood!* (Stage 8), *Rescue!* (Stage 9)

- Episodic stories: *The Stolen Crown Part 1* (Stage 6), *The Stolen Crown Part 2* (Stage 6)

1 Imitate: *Traction Man Is Here*

- The children need to fully understand and internalise the story before they move on to telling Pie's innovated story.

- Try to embed some of the key phrases and memorable language so children are familiar with the story structure.

- Keep reading and joining in as a class, saying the story together.

- Try retelling in groups or in pairs.

- Emphasise the episodic nature of the story as you retell it to highlight how the story is structured.

- If appropriate, use an enlarged copy of the *Traction Man Is Here* story map on Resource Sheet 4 for children to retell the story or draw your own.

 Use Resource Sheet 4 on page 63 to retell *Traction Man Is Here* as a class.

2 Innovate: Pie Corbett's story

- Tell the class that they are going to learn how to tell a new story, *Fraction Man.* It is similar to *Traction Man Is Here,* but some things have changed.

- Click on *Tell* to play the video of Pie Corbett telling the story of *Fraction Man* using his story map and actions. Encourage the class to join in.

- Replay the video a number of times. As the children become more confident, gradually turn down the volume so that they retell the story without Pie's voice.

- Ask the children to retell the story as a class, then in groups or pairs, before they have a go on their own.

- Practise using expression by rehearsing memorable lines.

- Retelling is not a memory game. Most children need to see a story map, do the actions and possibly use objects, to retell the story.

- An enlarged photocopy of the story map, or your own version of it, should always be displayed.

 Use Resource Sheet 5 on page 64 for children to use to retell *Fraction Man.* Some children may want to create their own story maps. Resource Sheet 6 on page 65 shows Pie's story script.

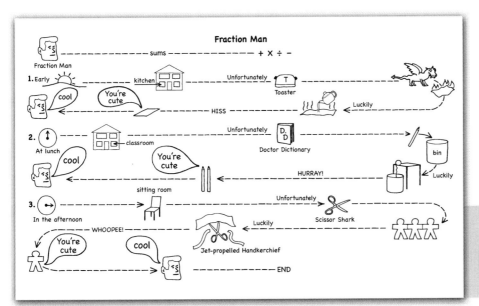

A story map of Pie's innovated story, *Fraction Man*

WRITE

1 Planning together

- Click on *Write* to use Pie's story map to help you invent a shared class story.

- Make appropriate changes and practise each one as you add them to the story map on screen or on a flip chart, so your own version develops.

- Ensure the children are involved in this process, using partner talk or mini whiteboards to compose their ideas.

- Ideas for changes include:

> ○ Create a new main character, e.g. a new superhero or heroine, a new sidekick, a new baddy.
>
> ○ Create new names, e.g. Traction Girl, Marvel Mouse, Wonder Brush.
>
> ○ Create new settings, e.g. the playground, the supermarket.
>
> ○ Create new adventures or 'rescues'.
>
> ○ Add verbs, e.g. squashed, explored.
>
> ○ Add adverbs, e.g. wearily, powerfully, bravely.
>
> ○ Invent expressions for your new hero/heroine.

- Retell the new story as a class, in groups and then in pairs.

2 Shared writing

- Once the children know the new class story, move into shared writing.

- As well as simple changes, try adding in extra details to embellish the story. This could be 'dropping in' words (adjectives) or adding whole sentences and chunks of text.

- Stick to a similar repetitive pattern to Pie's story.

> ○ Orally rehearse the story, then write and reread it.
>
> ○ Try to keep a 'flow' as you write.
>
> ○ Encourage children's suggestions for good words and ideas to use in the class story.
>
> ○ Use the word *said* throughout the shared story so that you can work together to improve this.
>
> ○ Draw the children's attention to the dialogue and ask the children to work in pairs using their mini whiteboards to come up with suitable synonyms to replace the word *said* in the story.
>
> ○ Tell the children that you want them to use other words for *said*.

3 Recording children creating their own stories

- Lead children through developing their own map based on this story.

- In pairs, encourage them to tell and retell their version before recording it.

- Work with groups, pairs or individual children to help them record stories at their own level.

> **Children can:**
>
> ○ dictate to an adult who scribes
> ○ record their story using a microphone
> ○ video their story with a digital camera
> ○ perform to a group
> ○ write a group text
>
> ○ write with support
> ○ write independently, with annotations in consultation with an adult
> ○ write independently.

4 Guided writing

Focus: select appropriate and effective vocabulary (AF7)

- Some children may need help with this focus and this session should only occur once the children have written some of their own story.

- Show the children the page where Traction Man saves the spoons. Ask the children to help you describe how Traction Man might have spoken (mumbled, shouted, laughed, etc).

- Model writing the dialogue, inserting the different synonyms for *said*. Talk about how these synonyms change *how* Traction Man speaks.

- Ask the children to find some dialogue in their stories and read it aloud to their partner. Can they say the dialogue in lots of different ways? *Which way works best?*

- Ask the children to use their mini whiteboards to improve their dialogue by using a synonym for *said* to show the reader how their hero and villain are speaking.

- You can differentiate this session for less confident and more confident children.

  o **Improve a group text which the children all contribute to, focusing on synonyms for *said* and replacing these in the children's writing.**

  o **Challenge the children to look at the dialogue they have written and improve it, as well as use synonyms for *said*.**

5 Assessing children's writing

Focus: select appropriate and effective vocabulary (AF7)

- Focus on the children's language choices and dialogue. More confident writers will use dialogue to move the action on and synonyms for *said* to create atmosphere, a sense of urgency and a voice for their character.

- Use *I can* statements to encourage children to evaluate their writing, for example: *I can write down what my characters say. I can use other words instead of 'said'.*

- All children can improve their dialogue by:

  o **Reading it aloud to a friend to make sure it makes sense.**

  o **Having a bank of synonyms for *said* to choose from and understanding what they mean.**

  o **Making sure their dialogue does not repeat action already described in the story. (The children walked up the mountain. "We walked up a big mountain," puffed Jake.)**

  o **Improving their dialogue through role-playing and oral rehearsal.**

✏ EXTENDED WRITING

1 Transform everyday objects into villains

- Look for the villains in the book and talk about what they really are (pillows, dishcloth, spade, toes, sock, a broom).
- Model turning an ordinary object into a villain. Remind the children to use capital letters for names.

 Use Resource Sheet 7 on page 66 to help children create their own villain from an everyday object.

2 Dialogue between Traction Man and his enemies

- Look through the book and highlight all the dialogue between Traction Man and his enemies. Talk about the use of speech bubbles.
- Encourage the children to act out some of the dialogue, giving the characters different voices.

- Model writing some dialogue between Traction Man and one of his enemies. Ask the children to have a go using mini whiteboards.

 Use Resource Sheet 8 on page 67 to help you write some dialogue for Traction Man and his enemies.

3 Advert for Traction Man toy

- Look at the cover of the book and the toy box on the first page. Discuss how the toy is described.
- Talk about what you would include in an advert to sell Traction Man as a toy.
- *What would you need to know about the toy?*

- Work together to create persuasive and descriptive phrases.

 Use Resource Sheet 9 on page 68 to help you design and write your advert for the Traction Man toy.

4 Comic strip of a new Traction Man adventure

- Some children may enjoy creating a comic strip to tell part of the Traction Man story or as another way to present their own stories.
- Use other comic strips and the pages in the book with speech bubbles as references before breaking up the Traction Man story into parts.

- Model using the speech bubbles to show dialogue.

Use Resource Sheet 10 on page 69 to help you create your own Traction Man comic strip.

Art

- Read and discuss the illustrations, for example look for references to wool in Gran's sitting room.

- Talk about the use of mixed media in the book and how it adds interest.

- Identify the different media used (fabrics, print, paper, paint, ink).

Design and Technology

- Look at the different outfits that Traction Man wears in the story.

- Design a new outfit for Traction Man for a space adventure.

- *What materials would be suitable in space? What special gadget could you create for him?*

Geography

- Talk about longer journeys around the country. Ask the children to find out where their relatives live.

- Look on a map to find where the children's relatives live.

- Identify which way they could travel if they went on this journey by car.

Maths

- Talk about the passage of time in the story and create a timeline for the events of the day.

- Make sure the children have access to a list of the key events.

- Use questions to order the main events of the day such as: *What meal happens before the sink underwater adventure? Which meal do they have at Granny's?*

Music

- Listen to some theme music used for superhero films and TV shows.

- Discuss what they have in common (large orchestration, heavy repeated beats, repeated phrases, often getting louder and then quieter).

- Create a theme tune for *Traction Man Is Here* using percussion and voices.

PE

- Use any available equipment to create a superhero obstacle race.

PSHE

- Talk about the presents that the family got from Granny. Look carefully at the illustrations of the family members' faces. Ask: *How do you think they feel about their present? How does Traction Man feel?*

- Talk about how it feels when you are disappointed, especially when you are given a present you don't like.

Role-play area

- Create a space where doll's furniture can be set. Provide some action heroes/heroines and dressing-up clothes for the dolls.

Science

- Talk about what materials would create the strongest rope for Traction Man to save the Spoons from the Broom.

- Explore the strength of different materials (cotton, wool, ribbon, string) and create a fair test to find out which is the strongest.

Check out the *Stories for Writing* Planning CD-ROM for week-by-week literacy plans, exciting cross-curricular ideas and extra resource sheets.

TRACTION MAN IS HERE

Pumpkin Soup

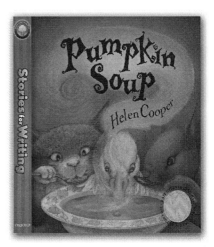

 **TALK**

- Before reading the book, ask the children to role-play cooking a cake. Encourage them to think about how to share the jobs. *Is everyone getting a fair turn?*

- Ask the children to role-play leaving out someone in their group. Talk about how it feels to be left out.

 Use Resource Sheet 1 on page 70 to record how it feels to fall out with a friend.

READ

1 Read the story together

- Select *Pumpkin Soup* on the CD-ROM.

- Click on *Read* to listen to the story being read from beginning to end without interruption.

- Enjoy the story and let the children discuss any aspect they are interested in.

- Let the children raise their own questions.

2 Book Talk

- Reread the story and savour it! Make sure it is on display whilst you explore these open questions. Encourage paired and group discussions. Interact with the text using the zoom, sticky notes and annotating tools to record the children's responses and ideas.

  - *How do you think the animals shared out the cooking jobs?*
  - *Tell me more about the reason for the big fight.*
  - *What would happen if Duck set up his own kitchen?*
  - *Who behaved badly?*
  - *Should Cat and Squirrel let Duck stir the soup?*

- Stop at points in the book and ask:

  - *What do you notice about how the friends make the music, the quilt and the soup? Why do you think the writer has done this?*
  - *What clue does the author give us that there is going to be a problem?*
  - *How would you describe the woods in this picture?*
  - *Could Duck have found better friends than Cat and Squirrel?*
  - *Who is sorry?*

 Use Resource Sheet 2 on page 71 for children to note a personal response to the story.

3 Explore the story

Setting: the woods

- Look at the opening pages. Ask the children to imagine they are going through a 'magic mirror' so they become part of the setting.

- What would they see or hear if they were there?

- Now look at Duck in the woods. Help the children compose an atmospheric piece to describe the setting of the woods at night.

Characters: the fight

- Look at the picture of the animals arguing. Role-play what they are saying.

- Drag a speech bubble to Cat and scribe the children's suggestions.

- Now drag a thought bubble to Cat and get the children to talk about what Cat might be thinking.

- Help the children notice that Cat may feel annoyed, sad or even hurt, but he doesn't say that he feels these things.

- Continue the process with the other two characters.

 Use Resource Sheet 3 on page 72 to make puppets to act out the fight. Talk about how the characters feel.

Word and Language Games: the opening

- Read the first page of the book together again. Talk about how it creates the setting, introduces the characters and makes an atmosphere.

- Draw out the main features of the opening and use these to model an innovated opening. For example, *Deep in the wood there's a tumble down cottage with apple trees in the garden. There's a smell of baked apple pie…*

- **Game: Change it.** Start by saying the opening, *Deep in the woods there's an old white cabin with pumpkins in the garden.* Ask a child to repeat the sentence, changing any word they wish. The next child changes another word, and so on.

- Write the final sentence up and see how much it has changed on its journey around the class!

Role-play and Drama

- Hot-seat the characters. Ask the children to get into pairs and think of questions to ask each character.

- Play music that evokes harmony and ask the children to act out making the pumpkin soup.

4 Guided/group and independent reading

- You will find ideas for parents/carers to use *Pumpkin Soup* with their child at home on the inside front cover of the storybook.

- You will find ideas for guided/group reading using *Pumpkin Soup* on the inside back cover of the storybook.

Deep in the woods there's an old white cabin with pumpkins in the garden. There's a good smell of soup, and at night, with luck, you might see a bagpiping Cat through the window, and a Squirrel with a banjo, and a small singing Duck.

An extract from *Pumpkin Soup*, by Helen Cooper, with kind permission from Random House Children's Books

5 Reading as a Writer

Return to the book and use it to explore the questions below, beginning to think about what might be needed to create your own version.

Plot

- Discuss with the children the kind of story *Pumpkin Soup* is. It is a friendship story with a fight. It is circular; it begins and ends in the same place.

- *What else could the animals fight about?* They could fight about: other chores, gardening, the type of music they make, etc.

- *How else could the story end?* Duck might not say sorry, the others might not want him back, everything could go back to normal, etc.

Setting

- *Where is the story set?* In an old white cabin in a wood.

- *Where else could it be set?* In a small beach hut by the seaside, in a flat in a city, in a tree-house in an orchard.

Character

- *How many main characters are there in Pumpkin Soup?* There are three – Duck, Squirrel and Cat.

- Discuss how Duck wants to change the way the three friends make soup and this causes all the characters to fall out.

Language

- Reread the part of the story where Duck is found. Look at how the friends react.

- *Are there any other words that could be used to describe how the friends felt when they all returned?* Cat and Squirrel were: relieved, overjoyed, delighted, thrilled. Duck was: happy, contented, satisfied.

- Innovate on the lyrical and figurative sentences to help embed these patterns, e.g. *Deep in the woods there's an old wooden hut.*

6 Other stories to read

Friendship stories

- *Meggie Moon* by Elizabeth Baguley
- *It's a George Thing* by David Bedford
- *Little Beauty* by Anthony Browne
- *Sylvia and Bird* by Catherine Rayner

Stories written by Helen Cooper

- *Delicious*
- *Dog Biscuit*
- *A Pipkin of Pepper*
- *The Bear Under the Stair*

7 Links to Oxford Reading Tree classic stories Stages 6–9

- Food: *The Big Breakfast* (Stage 7)
- Friends: *The Finest in the Land* (Stage 9)
- Day and night: *A Fright in the Night* (Stage 6), *The Power Cut* (Stage 7)

PUMPKIN SOUP

 **TELL**

1 Imitate: *Pumpkin Soup*

- The children need to fully understand and internalise the story before they move on to telling Pie's innovated story.

- Join in as a class with reading the story.

- Rehearse and chant memorable parts.

- Try retelling the story in your own words.

- Emphasise the actions as you retell the story to highlight what the animals are doing.

- If appropriate, use an enlarged copy of the *Pumpkin Soup* story map on Resource Sheet 4 for children to retell the story in their own words or draw your own version.

 Use Resource Sheet 4 on page 73 to retell *Pumpkin Soup* as a class.

2 Innovate: Pie Corbett's story

- Tell the class that they are going to learn how to tell a new story, *Time for Tea*. It is similar to *Pumpkin Soup*, but some things have changed.

- Click on *Tell* to play the video of Pie Corbett telling the story of *Time for Tea* using his story map and actions. Encourage the whole class to join in.

- Replay the video a number of times. As the children become more confident, gradually turn down the volume so that they retell the story without Pie's voice.

- Ask the children to retell the story as a class, then in groups or pairs, before they have a go on their own.

- Retelling is not a memory game. Most children will need to see a story map, do the actions and possibly use objects, to retell the story clearly.

- An enlarged photocopy of the story map, or your own version of it, should always be displayed.

 Use Resource Sheet 5 on page 74 to retell *Time for Tea*. Some children may want to create their own story maps. Resource Sheet 6 on page 75 shows Pie's story script.

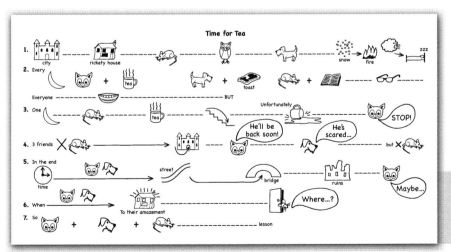

A story map of Pie's innovated story, *Time for Tea*

1 Planning together

- Click on *Write* to use Pie's story map to help you invent a shared class story.

- Make appropriate changes and practise each one as you add them to the story map on screen or on a flip chart. In this way your own version of the story will gradually develop.

- Ensure the children are involved in this process, using partner talk or mini whiteboards to compose their ideas.

- Ideas for changes include:

  - Create new characters, e.g. a badger, a chicken and a rabbit.
  - Create the shared activity, e.g. making biscuits, making music.
  - Create a new problem, e.g. one character wants to swap jobs, one wants to do something new.
  - Add feelings, e.g. angry, lonely, annoyed, unwelcome.
  - Add similes, e.g. the moon was like a wisp of smoke.

- Retell the new story as a class, in groups and then in pairs.

2 Shared writing

- Once the children know the new class story, move into shared writing.

- As well as simple changes, try adding in extra details to embellish the story. This could be 'dropping in' words (adjectives) or adding whole sentences and chunks of text.

- Craft the story and try using memorable and lyrical sentences.

- Take suggestions as the story develops and encourage the children to choose their words with care.

  - Focus on descriptive words that create the atmosphere. Model choosing words to make the house seem cosy and the woods scary.
  - Involve the children in the process of choosing words and phrases to create atmosphere through partner talk and by using their mini whiteboards to record their ideas.
  - Tell the children that you will be looking out for how they create atmosphere in their writing. Talk about 'seeing the story' in your head.

3 Recording children creating their own stories

- Lead children through developing their own map based on this story.

- In pairs, encourage them to tell and retell their version before recording it.

- Work with groups, pairs or individual children to help them record stories at their own level.

Children can:

- dictate to an adult who scribes
- record their story using a microphone
- video their story with a digital camera
- perform to a group
- write a group text

- write with support
- write independently, with annotations in consultation with an adult
- write independently.

④ Guided writing

Focus: write imaginative, interesting and thoughtful texts (AF1)

- Some children may need help with this focus and this session should only occur once the children have written some of their own story.

- Help children to find places where similes could be added by using 'like' or 'as … as'.

- Create similes for the moon, stars or the sound of the wind in the tree.

- You can differentiate this for less confident and more confident children.

  - o Work on a group description of the woods, to include a simile.

  - o Challenge the children to use the senses of sound, sight, smell and touch in their descriptions.

⑤ Assessing children's writing

Focus: write imaginative, interesting and thoughtful texts (AF1)

- Focus on how the children control their descriptions. Is it a sequence of simple sentences describing the setting visually or a linked set of sounds, images and feelings that builds the setting? More confident writers will use the senses to build a vivid description. The use of similes also shows a sense of control and an idea of imagery.

- Use *I can* statements to encourage children to evaluate their writing, for example: *I can use good describing words.*

- All children can improve their descriptions by:

  - o Using words that create sounds, for example rustle, crackle, snap, etc.

  - o Using words to show how large the setting is compared to their character, for example, *The huge trees loomed over the tiny duck …*

  - o Using short sentences to create pace.

  - o Putting a verb at the beginning of a sentence, for example, *Crack, the branches creaked above Duck.*

  - o Using similes to build a picture for the reader.

EXTENDED WRITING

1 Recipe for pumpkin soup

- If possible help a small group of children make some pumpkin soup and record the different stages. Alternatively, role-play the stages.
- Enlarge Resource Sheet 7 and work out the order of the pictures together. Discuss what instruction you could write under each picture.

- Children work independently or in groups to write a recipe for pumpkin soup and a set of simple instructions.

 Use Resource Sheet 7 on page 76 to sequence instructions for making pumpkin soup.

2 House rules

- Work in a group to discuss what helps people get on with each other. Talk about the class rules. *What do our rules help us to do?*
- *What rules would work well for the animals? How could Duck be helped?*

- Help the children compose clear rules for the friends that are easy to follow.

 Use Resource Sheet 8 on page 77 for children to create a list of rules for the three friends.

3 Onomatopoeia Poems

- Collect words from the book that make sound effects (onomatopoeic words): ker-plonk, clattered, squeaked, snapped, whoops, squabble, tok.
- Work together to create a sound scape of words to make the sound of a fight and the sound of a scary wood at night.

 Use Resource Sheet 9 on page 78 for children to collect words to help them write their own onomatopoeic poem.

4 Description of the woods at night

- Look at the cabin on the first page. Model using similes to describe the setting and then ask the children to have a go. For example, *The moon is like a gentle smile, The trees are like giant embraces.*
- It helps if you draw the object, for example the moon could be drawn like a slice of melon.

- Now show the pictures of the woods at night and model similes for the setting that enhance the scary atmosphere. For example, *The trees are like looming giants, The path is like a twisted snake.*

 Use Resource Sheet 10 on page 79 as a stimulus to write similes to describe two different settings.

CROSS-CURRICULAR ACTIVITIES

Art

- Look at the pumpkin house on the first page. Make pumpkin houses from squashes and pumpkins that have been carved out or make papier-maché pumpkin houses.
- Look closely at the pictures of the pumpkins in the pumpkin patch. Visit an allotment, the school vegetable patch or bring in pumpkins and pumpkin leaves for the children to draw and paint.

Design and Technology

- Look at the pages with Duck's Kitchen.
- Design an attractive menu for Duck's new restaurant.

Geography

- *Pumpkin Soup* is set in woodland. Visit or research a wood close to your school. Find out what types of plants grow there and what animals live in that habitat.
- Find out how the woods are used and what things can be made from trees.

Maths

- Notice the shapes in the pictures and try to describe them. Look at how the window is made of different shapes that fit together.
- Make tessellations using different shapes. Work out which shapes tessellate and which don't.

Music

- Learn some parts of the story by heart (the beginning, the fight, the scary woods and the reunion) and say or sing them as a class chorally.
- Create sounds and rhythms to go with the words that add to the atmosphere.

PE

- Work in groups of three to create strong balances.

PSHE

- Talk about how people change. Remind the children about when they started school. Encourage them to reflect on how they have grown and changed.
- Make a list of what they could do in their first year at school and compare it to what they can do now.
- Celebrate the children's achievements and consider how they embraced changes.

Role-play area

- Create a 'cabin' area for the children to use for role-play.
- Darken the hall and pretend to walk through the forest at night!
- Use shoe boxes to create mini worlds for new stories.

Science

- Plant vegetable seeds and record how they grow.
- Plan the ingredients that you need for a healthy vegetable soup.

Check out the *Stories for Writing* Planning CD-ROM for week-by-week literacy plans, exciting cross-curricular ideas and extra resource sheets.

PUMPKIN SOUP

Name ....

Build a fairy

Name: ....

Job title: ....

Special powers: ....

Clothing: ....

Habitat (where they can be found): ....

○ Talk about the different types of fairies at the top of the page.

○ Ask the children to make up a new fairy. What will it look like, what job will it do, where will it live?

○ Ask the children to draw a picture of their new fairy and fill in the details.

Name ....

How did I do?

Dave and the Tooth Fairy

1. What was Dave's problem?

   ....

   ....

2. If you got some money from the Tooth Fairy, what would you spend it on?

   ....

   ....

3. Draw Grandad's face when he saw his teeth under Dave's pillow.

   ┌──┐
   │   │
   │   │
   │   │
   │   │
   │   │
   └──┘

4. Have you ever lost a tooth? Write about it.

   ....

   ....

o Ask children to complete a personal response to the story.

o Encourage children to discuss their ideas first with a partner.

This may be reproduced for class use within purchaser's institution

Name ....

Character profiles

What does Dave want?	Who is Dave's friend?
....	....

Describe Dave in four words.

....

What is Afiya's problem?	What does Afiya want?
....	....

Write two interesting facts about Afiya.

....

○ Ask the children to find out about the main characters and fill in their profiles.

Adjectives

Dave and the Tooth Fairy Resource Sheet 4

1. It was his .... sneeze.

   biggest   most enormous   largest

2. He found .... comb.

   a huge   an enormous   a massive

3. It was her .... flight ever.

   fastest   speediest   quickest

4. David flew his kite:

   his .... kite ever.

   biggest   largest   most gigantic

---

o Talk about the comb on page 4 of the story. How does the adjective help us to imagine what it looks like?

o Ask the children to complete the sentences by looking at the pictures and choosing an adjective from the list.

Story map for *Dave and the Tooth Fairy*

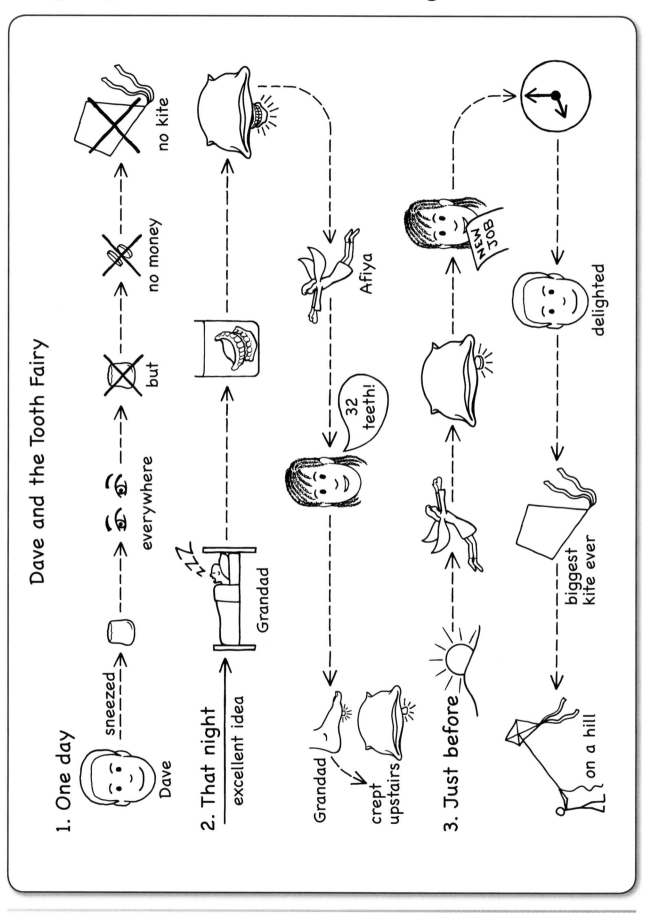

○ This is a story map for *Dave and the Tooth Fairy*. Display an enlarged version in the classroom as you retell the story.

Pie's story map

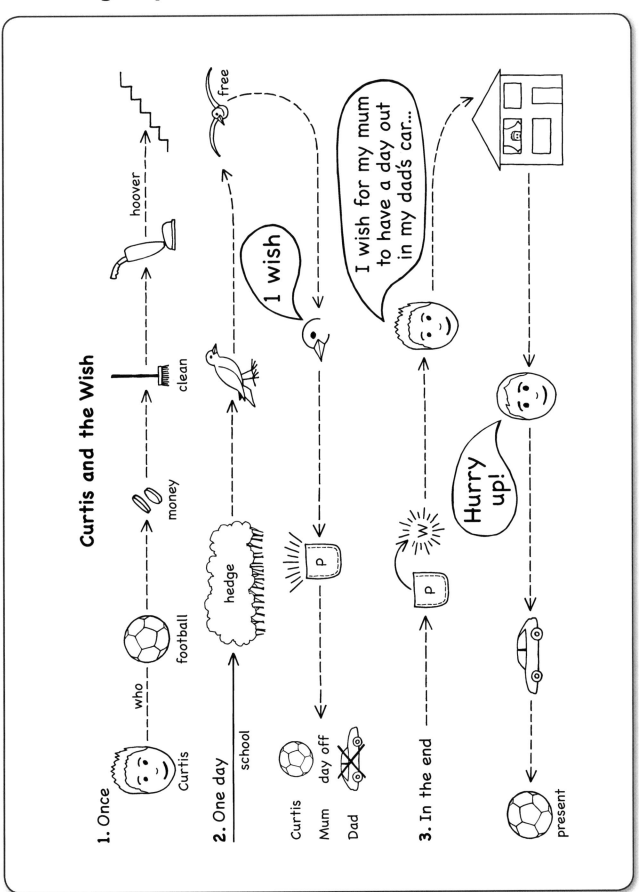

o Display this story map in the classroom when the children are ready to join in retelling Pie's innovated story.

Curtis and the Wish

Now once upon a time, there was a little boy called Curtis who wanted a football.

He saved all his pocket money.

He helped his mum clean the floor and his dad hoover the stairs.

One day, Curtis was on his way to school when he saw something trapped inside the hedge.

To his amazement, he found a golden bird.

Of course, Curtis set it free.

"For setting me free I can grant you one wish," said the golden bird.

Curtis caught the wish and put it into his pocket. It was small and shiny.

He kept the wish a secret, and thought very carefully about what he wanted to wish for. He only had one wish.

Now, Curtis wanted a football but his mum hadn't had a day off work for ages and his dad's old car had broken down. But Curtis only had the one wish. He thought all day about it.

And then, in the end, he decided what he could wish for.

Carefully, he took the wish out of his pocket and he whispered, "I wish for my mum to have a day's outing in Dad's car."

From his bedroom window, Curtis looked down and he could see his mum going out with his dad to get into the car to go off for an outing together.

"Hey, hurry up!" called Dad, beckoning to Curtis.

When Curtis ran down the stairs and went outside his dad opened up the back door of the car. Curtis climbed in. To his amazement there was a present there, wrapped up.

Curtis knew immediately what it was because it was round and just the same size... as a football.

Dave and the Tooth Fairy Resource Sheet 7

○ Use this script to help you lead the children in retelling *Curtis and the Wish*.

Name ....

Under my old sofa I found...

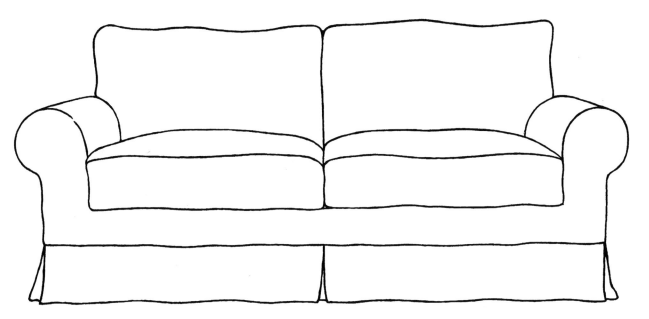

Under my old sofa I found...

....

....

....

....

....

....

o After describing the objects you brought into the classroom, ask the children to write their list poem, selecting some of the objects.

o Encourage them to think of new adjectives to describe each object.

57

Name ....

I want to be a Tooth Fairy!

Dave and the Tooth Fairy Resource Sheet 9

TOOTH FAIRY JOB DESCRIPTION

🪄 Must be able to keep a secret.

🪄 Should have flying licence.

🪄 Needs own wings.

🪄 Must like children.

🪄 Must be able to find small things.

🪄 Should be good at lifting pillows!

What can you .... ?

Have you ever .... ?

Do you know how to .... ?

How would you .... ?

What would you do if .... ?

○ Collect ideas for questions that the children could ask each other in an interview for the Tooth Fairy job.

○ Children can then write their own questions and interview their partner.

Name ....

How did I do?

Afiya's diary

Dear Diary,

What a night! I flew out through the beautiful night

sky to collect a tooth, but when I got to Dave's house...

....

....

....

....

....

....

....

○ Talk about what happened when Afiya got to Dave's house. Ask the children to share their ideas about how she felt.

○ Ask the children to pretend to be Afiya and write an entry in her diary.

Name ....

Create your own superhero

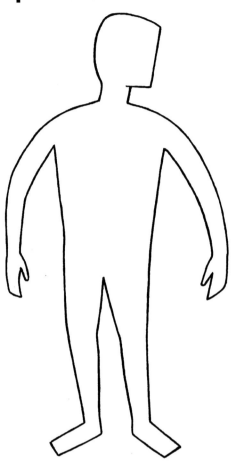

My superhero's name:

....

My superhero's special powers:

....

....

....

○ Ask the children to create their own superhero.

○ Ask them to choose a name and list their special powers.

Name ....

Traction Man Is Here

1. When I first read the story I thought

....

....

....

2. My favourite character was ....

because ....

....

....

3. The scariest part was ....

....

....

4. The best picture was ....

....

....

....

o Ask children to complete a personal response to the story.

o Encourage children to discuss their ideas first with a partner.

Name ....

Powerful words for *said*

| cheered | shouted | cried | laughed |

1. Write *how* the farm animals thanked Traction Man.

"Hooray for Traction Man!"

....

the farm animals.

2. Write *how* the Dollies thanked Traction Man.

"How can we repay you?"

....

....

3. Write *what* the Spoons said to thank Traction Man.

   Write *how* the Spoons thanked Traction Man.

o Look at the words for 'said' in the box. Talk about which word is most appropriate for how the characters spoke to Traction Man.

o Ask the children to fill in the dialogue for the characters and to write alternative words for 'said'. Do the first one together.

Story map for *Traction Man Is Here*

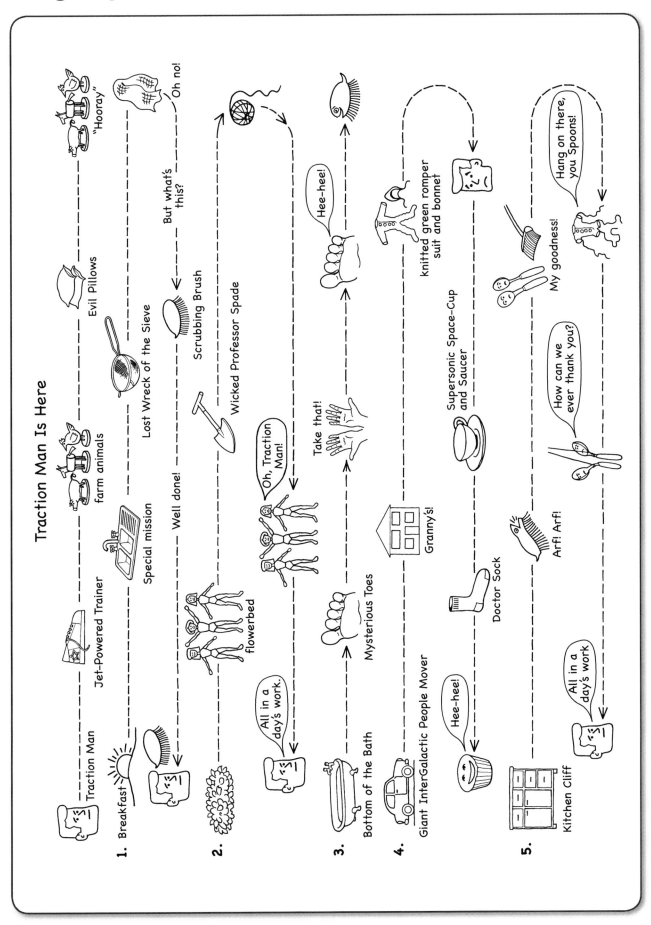

o This is a story map for *Traction Man Is Here*. Display an enlarged version in the classroom as you retell the story.

Pie's story map

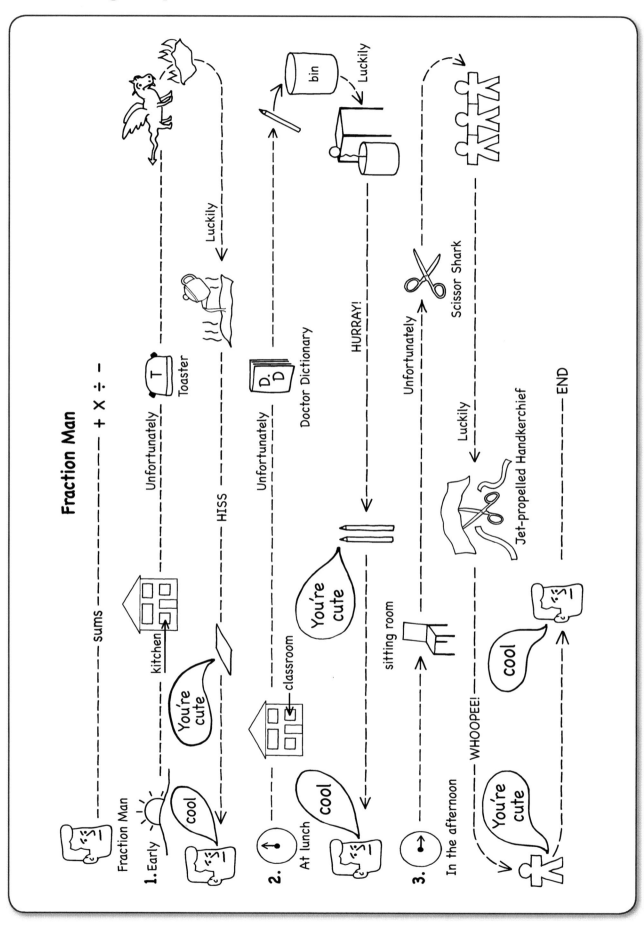

○ Display this story map in the classroom when the children are ready to join in retelling Pie's innovated story.

Fraction Man

This is a day in the life of Fraction Man.

Fraction Man can do sums.

He can add up, he can multiply, he can divide and he can take away.

Adventure No. 1

Early in the morning, Fraction Man is in the kitchen.

Unfortunately, the Toaster has turned into a deadly DRAGON and is breathing fire all over the dish cloth.

Luckily, Fraction Man swoops down on his Supersonic Teapot and pours tea all over the flames.

HISS!

"You're so cute," murmurs the dish cloth.

"Ahh, that's cool," says Fraction Man. "I'm off to take away a take-away."

Adventure No. 2

At lunch time, Fraction Man is in the classroom.

Unfortunately, the evil Dr Dictionary has stolen all the pencils and trapped them in the bin.

Luckily, Fraction Man finds a ball of string, climbs down into the bin and rescues all the pencils.

HURRAY!

"You're so cute," chime the pencils.

"Ahh, that's cool," replies Fraction Man. "Don't worry, I'm off now to count the number of leaves on a tree."

Adventure No. 3

In the afternoon, Fraction Man is in the sitting room.

Unfortunately, the villainous Scissor Shark is about to cut up rough with the paper dollies who are all holding hands.

Luckily, Fraction Man throws a Jet-Propelled Handkerchief over the Scissor Shark and then ties it up in ribbons.

WHOOPEE!

"You're so cute," sing the paper dollies.

"Well, that's cool," says Fraction Man. "I'm off to kick a cuboid."

Now that's the end of the Amazing Adventures of Fraction Man – unless you know any better!

Traction Man Is Here Resource Sheet 6

○ Use this script to help you lead the children in retelling *Fraction Man*.

Name ....

Create a villain

My villain

My villain's name:

....

My villain's special powers are:

....

....

○ Talk about what a villain does and what powers they sometimes have.

○ Ask the children to draw their villain from one of the everyday objects, think of an evil name and list their special powers.

Name ....

Speech bubbles

You were caught red-ink handed Pew the Poison Pen!

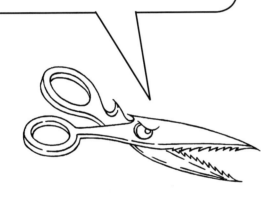

Ha! I have trapped you! You are doomed!

Watch out! The super heated porridge is about to blow!

○ Model writing what Traction Man would say to the villain in the first speech bubble, using stereotypical language a superhero might use.

○ Ask the children to fill in the speech bubbles, supporting as appropriate.

Name ....

Traction Man advert

○ Talking about what features Traction Man could have, for example *Traction Man with even more dazzle!*

○ Help the children to scribe a new feature for Traction Man on the front of the box, and to finish designing it.

How did I do?

Comic strip

- o Look at some comic strips and talk about how they are different to a normal book. Talk about the type of language used, for example *Pow!* and *Wow!*

- o Model filling in the comic strip template, using an episode from *Fraction Man*.

- o Help the children to fill in the comic strip using one of the adventures in their own superhero story.

Name ....

Friendship

When I fight with my friends I feel

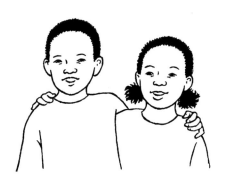

....

....

....

....

When I fall out with my friends I feel

....

....

....

....

When we make up I feel

....

....

....

....

○ Ask the children to complete the sentences about how they feel when they fight, fall out and make up with their friends.

Name ....

Pumpkin Soup

1. When I read the story I thought ....

....

....

2. My favourite character was .... because

....

....

3. The scariest part for me was ....

....

....

4. The best picture was ....

....

....

o Ask children to complete a personal response to
   the story.

o Encourage children to discuss their ideas first with
   a partner.

This may be reproduced for class use within purchaser's institution

Name ....

How did I do?

Puppet show

Use the puppets to act out the fight in *Pumpkin Soup*.

o Ask the children to cut out the pictures (with help from an adult). Glue the pictures to cardboard and then attach to sticks to make puppets.

o After the children have created their puppets, allow them time to practise acting out the fight in the story.

Story map for *Pumpkin Soup*

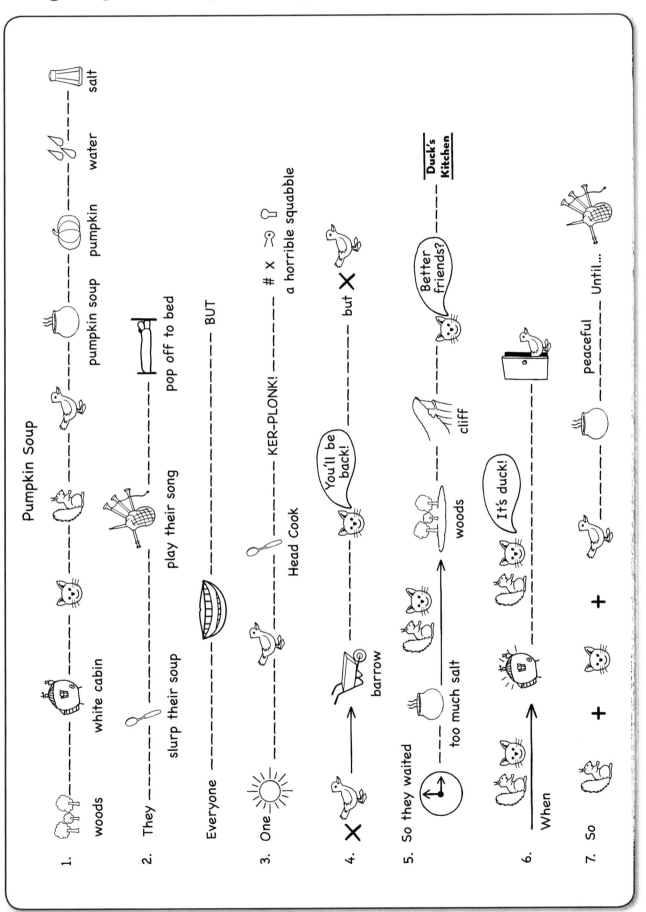

Pumpkin Soup

1. woods — white cabin — play their song — pumpkin soup — pumpkin — water — salt

2. They — slurp their soup — pop off to bed

3. Everyone — BUT — One — KER-PLONK! — Head Cook — # x — a horrible squabble

4. X — barrow — You'll be back! — but X

5. So they waited — too much salt — woods — cliff — Better friends? — **Duck's Kitchen**

6. When — It's duck! — peaceful — Until...

7. So — + — +

○ This is a story map for *Pumpkin Soup*. Display an enlarged version in the classroom as you retell the story.

Pie's story map

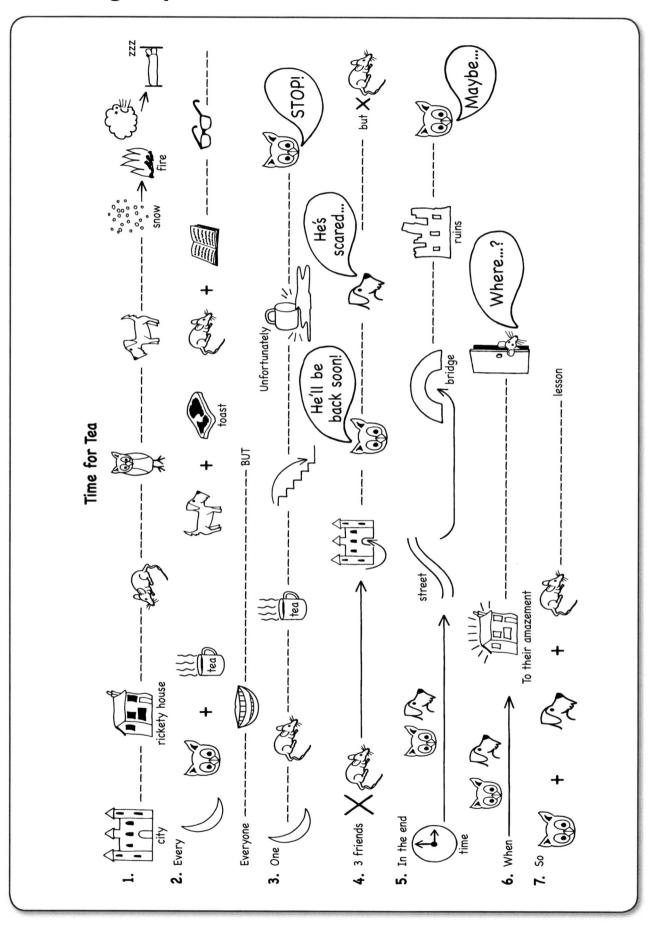

o Display this story map in the classroom when the children are ready to join in retelling Pie's innovated story.

Time for Tea

Deep in an ancient city is a rickety house.

In the rickety house there are not one, not two, but three friends – Mouse, Owl and Dog.

When the snow falls, they light the fire.

When the wind blows, they snuggle up in their beds.

Every night time Owl makes a cup of tea, Dog makes toast on the fire and then Mouse reads to them all.

He scampers off and puts his little glasses on, scuttles up and down the page reading to Owl and Dog.

Everyone is happy, or so it seems.

BUT

One night when the others were fast asleep, Mouse decided to make some tea.

He went downstairs. He got the teapot, he put the kettle on and began to brew up some tea. Unfortunately, he knocked the cup onto the floor – smash, crack! He spilt the milk everywhere.

"Stop making that tea," shouted Owl. "That is my job."

Soon, the three friends began to squabble and argue and shout at each other.

"I'm not staying here" said Mouse. "You never let me do anything at all."
Mouse went out of the house into the dark streets.

"I'm not staying, I'm going!" he called.

"Hmm, don't worry, he'll be back soon," said Owl.

"He's scared of the dark," growled Dog.

But Mouse did not come back.

Time ticked by.

In the end, Owl and Dog went out to find Mouse.

They searched the shadowy streets.

They searched under the old bridge.

They searched in the crumbling ruins.

"Maybe a nightmare has stolen him," said Owl.

Dog's bottom lip began to tremble.

"Perhaps we should have let Mouse make the tea. Perhaps we should have helped him."

Well, when they'd looked everywhere, the two friends decided they would have to go back to the rickety house without Mouse. Sadly, they trudged through the dark streets.

To their amazement, the lights were on in the rickety house. They stood for a moment. Then Owl swooped up to the door and Dog barked. Mouse poked his little head out of the door.

"Where have you been?" he asked. "*Where have you been?* I hope you weren't too worried. Come along, breakfast is ready on the table and I've made some tea."

So the three friends sat down to eat and all of them had learned a little lesson.

Not just one of them, not just two of them, but all three.

o Use this script to help you lead the children in retelling *Time for Tea*.

This may be reproduced for class use within purchaser's institution

Name ....

How to make pumpkin soup

You will need:

....

....

....

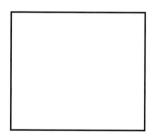 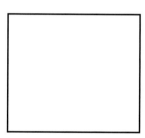 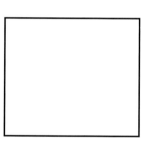 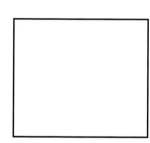

What to do:

1. First ....

2. Next ....

3. Then ....

4. Finally ....

○ Help the children to list the ingredients for pumpkin soup.

○ Allow them time to cut out and order the pictures.

○ The children then write their own instructions for making pumpkin soup.

Name ....

Rules for friendship

....

....

....

....

....

....

....

o Ask the children to think of some rules which they think are important for keeping friends, for example learning to share.

o Ask the children to order their list of rules according to which they think are the most important.

Pumpkin Soup Resource Sheet 9

Onomatopoeic poetry

snarl

yowl

- o Discuss the example above. Can the children think of any other onomatopoeic words for the fight?

- o Work together to come up with some words to describe the wood at night.

- o Using the onomatopoeic sound words discussed, model writing a poem about one of the settings.

- o Ask the children to choose a setting and create a poem of their own.

Name ....

Describing different settings

....

....

....

....

....

....

....

....

....

....

○ Ask the children to look at the pictures and describe what is in each setting. Encourage them to come up with their own similes to evoke the atmosphere of each setting.

○ Model some examples, such as *The sea was like a sparkling diamond. The trees branches were like grasping hands.*

This may be reproduced for class use within purchaser's institution

Notes